A Father to You

*"I will be a Father to you and you will be my sons
and daughters"
(2 Corinthians 6:18 NIV)*

A signpost to the heart of the perfect Father who
wants to be a Father to YOU

A Biblical perspective of experiencing God as
Father

Mark Gyde

Dedicated to my four children: Frances, Hilary, Hannah and John whom I trust will forgive me for all the mistakes I have made.

And to my wife and best friend, Fiona, for her support, encouragement and help with editing this book. And of course for her unfailing love.

I love you all.....

Contents

Foreword

I am honoured to endorse Mark's new book 'A Father To You'. This collection of topics on the Fatherheart of God will serve as a signpost for you to come to know your heavenly Father in a way you might not have thought possible before.

Mark lays a solid Biblical foundation on the revelation of Father's love and he continues to build on that foundation throughout the book. You will find many inspiring nuggets of truth that will help you comprehend the amazing love that God has for you.

This book will also help you understand some of the things that may hinder you from going deeper into love and provide practical ways to address those issues. Mark is very thorough in dealing with many of these hindrances and he continually provides helpful signposts to point us back in the direction of our Father's love. I am confident that this book will help you journey from orphan belief systems to the place of resting in your identity as a beloved child of God.

'A Father To You' comes from a place in Mark's heart where he has tried and tested its truths in his own life. It is really a summary of his own life story with his heavenly Father, and I would highly recommend that you read it. As you do, I believe that you will move closer and closer to the love you have been looking for all your life.

Barry Adams - Author of "The Father's Love Letter" *and creator of* Fatherheart.tv

Introduction

A Father To You

"I will be a Father to you and you will be my sons and daughters"
(2 Corinthians 6:18 NIV)

I am very privileged to have four lovely children. All our friends know that I am their father. Their friends know that I am their father; school teachers, bank managers, work colleagues – they too know I am the father of these four children. Many people know that I am a father but only four people know it intimately. Those four are my children. They have lived with me and shared my hopes, dreams and failures. They know what I like and what I am like. They know what I like doing, where I like going and the sort of food I like. They know what makes me cross and what makes me happy. They have experienced my care, my love and my provision. They are my three daughters and my son.

It is just the same in the church. Most people know that God is a Father in much the same way as people outside of my family know that I am a father. They know that fact because they have been taught it or because they see it in Scripture. But they may not have experienced it. Too many people in the church only have a theology of God as a Father but few have come to experience him as a Father to them.

They are like my acquaintances; they know that I am a father but they do not experience my fathering. God's heart is that we come to experience him as Father. God, our Father, wants us to have a heart of sonship and to experience his love as Jesus did. After all, when we became Christians we became children of God (John 1:12).

This book is a journey of discovery. Its intention is not only to give a biblical perspective on the nature and heart of the Father but also to help you experience his perfect love and find the Father you may have been looking for all your life. I would ask you to read this book not to gain head knowledge but as a guide to lead you into a deeper personal revelation and experience of God as your Father.

I hope that reading this book will prompt you to take time to rest in God's loving presence and allow his love to fill your heart, for as Dr Larry Crabb said, "Understanding the love of God does not require a classroom lecture but a long bath"[1]. How true!

As you read, may the eyes of your heart be opened and the ears of your spirit tuned in to hear the voice of One calling you, the One who has always been Father and who wants to be a Father to you.

Notes:
1. Larry Crabb in He Loves Me by Wayne Jacobsen

Chapter 1

God Has Always Been Father

"In the beginning...."
(John 1:1 and Genesis 1:1)

Where does our story begin?

We all know something of our family background - the place we were born or the houses we lived in and the people we knew. We know our brothers and sisters, our parents, our grandparents, our families and friends. We have childhood recollections of holidays or Sunday afternoon walks, of school and of growing up. Mostly, we remember the good things. But in all of us there are areas of pain that we would rather shut out and forget. There are also memories of painful events which have shaped us as much as the good times.

I look back on my childhood with many fond memories. Only the other day my family was talking about the Sunday afternoons when we would all cram into my uncle's car and go off into the countryside around Birmingham, where I spent my first few years. We reckoned there were eight of us in the car – not something we would do nowadays! Whenever we saw horse muck on the road, we would shout, "Uncle Hedley's bucket!". My uncle always carried a bucket and spade for such eventualities so he could scoop up the organic matter and take it back for his garden.

I was very fortunate to have excellent parents who cared for me and my sisters. We were not well off but our enjoyment of family life was not dependent on money. I have three sisters; one is older than I am and two younger. When I was ten (by which time we had moved from Birmingham to Oxfordshire) my father was killed in a car accident. I guess it felt like the bottom had fallen out of our lives. It was an event which shaped the future of our family at every level. I can only pay tribute to the wonderful way in which my mother continued to bring us up and how she poured herself out for us all.

I know that many people reading this may have been less fortunate than I was. Family life may be something you are keen to shut out and move away from. It may have been the source of pain and broken relationships. Many hearts may have been broken in such circumstances and the disappointment from that brokenness may have become a bitter foundation for the future.

Our individual stories shape our view of God. Bad experiences with a natural father can make it difficult to experience God as a loving heavenly Father. However, having a good family can also make it difficult to come close to God as we may not perceive any need of him. God can be a distant figure whatever our family background.

However much we remember of our early days, that is not the beginning of our story. It begins way back in time, in fact, before time began.

Before the foundation of the world God had each one of us in mind (Psalm 139:16). He knew all about us. He knew where we would be born and where we would live (Acts 17:26). The prophet Jeremiah was told that God knew him before he had been formed in the womb. He knows each of us intimately and more importantly he has made us in order to have friendship with him!

So, our story begins in the beginning.

In the Bible "in the beginning" features prominently on two occasions. Genesis 1:1 states "In the beginning God created the Heavens and the earth". We read how he created light and darkness, seas and dry land, sun, moon and stars, plants and trees, animals of all kinds and finally - the crowning glory - he comes to earth and out of the dust he forms man in his own image.

The second "in the beginning" actually precedes the one in Genesis as it tells of a time before the foundation of the world. John 1:1 tells us "In the beginning was the Word, and the Word was with God, and the Word was God". This is the time before time! Later in John's gospel we learn a little more about this time and what was happening. We see who was involved and what had always been intended for us. At the end of Jesus' life he prays for his disciples and those that will follow:

> *"I pray also for those who will believe in me through their message, that all of them may be one, Father, just as you are in me and I am in you. May*

they also be in us so that the world may believe that you have sent me. I have given them the glory that you gave me, that they may be one as we are one: I in them and you in me. May they be brought to complete unity to let the world know that you sent me and have loved them even as you have loved me.

"Father, I want those you have given me to be with me where I am, and to see my glory, the glory you have given me because you loved me before the creation of the world.

"Righteous Father, though the world does not know you, I know you, and they know that you have sent me. I have made you known to them, and will continue to make you known in order that the love you have for me may be in them and that I myself may be in them." (John 17:20-26 NIV)

In these verses we are given a glimpse of eternity. We are told what it was like before the creation of the world and we are told about our glorious future.

From before the creation of the world there has been a beautiful unity and harmony in the Trinity. Relationships between Father, Son and Spirit were based totally on love. There was no element of control or manipulation. There was no fear or insecurity, nor were there any divided loyalties. The Trinity was complete in itself. It was so complete, in fact, that God did not need creation as an object to love. Yet, Jesus prays that we will enjoy and be drawn into the same unity and the same relationship which the Trinity enjoys. Jesus' prayer is, quite simply, that we would be like him!

For us, love is a characteristic, but for God it is who he is. It is his very nature. Whatever God does, he does out of love, for love and through love. It was Jesus who came to introduce us to this love.

So the beginning of the story is perfect love. Everything in creation was made by love and for love. Love was the foundation of the world. Love was the essence of the life that was breathed into us. As the song says "It's love that makes the world go round"[1].

Our story begins when a loving Father breathed love into the human race. It was what we should have enjoyed forever.

But, we know the story. Unfortunately, the world did not stay as it had been made. Adam and his wife began by enjoying the same perfect relationship with the Father that the Trinity enjoyed. They walked together in the cool of the day. They enjoyed being sought out by their Father. Theirs was a relationship we all desire but find so hard to achieve. We do not know how much later it was when that fateful choice was made. But one day they chose to walk away from the Father's covering and seek independence.

And God let them.

I guess we have all wondered why he let that happen. Of course God could have stopped them.

He could have ignored it or he could have struck them down and started again.

So why did he let it happen?

God acted entirely consistently with his nature. If he had prevented that fateful act then his love would have become controlling. Essentially he would have been forcing them to love him. That is not love. Love is a gift. It is something we give from the heart; it is drawn out of us. We can never be forced to love. God understands love, because after all, he is LOVE. He knows what real love is and he knew that by stopping that act of independence he would have broken the relationship between us and him. It would have taken away the spontaneity and freewill from which love should flow. It would have redefined love forever. God simply could not do that.

We have a cat called Muf (short for Mufasa) who likes sleeping on our bed at night. Most nights he will come in and nestle into a comfortable place at the foot of the bed. As the night goes on he may move up a bit closer. Many a time we have woken to find him right between us! However, we cannot *force* him to sleep on our bed at night. If we find him wandering around the house at bedtime and pick him up to put him on the bed, then invariably he jumps off. He comes back in his own time. As much as we like having him on the bed we cannot make him stay there against his will. As much as God wants to have a relationship of love with us, he cannot make us love him against our will. That would be force not love.

When God drove Adam and Eve from the garden and allowed them to live with the consequences of their decision, it was an act of love. God knew that if they remained there it would be possible for them to eat from the tree of life and live forever. Such eternal life would be eternity without God; it would mean being permanently separated from the love God intended. It would be eternity spent living in a broken state, aware of their vulnerability and weakness. God, in his love, could not bear that to happen and so they were driven away. Even in that banishment we see a tender act of fatherly love. When Adam and his wife became aware of their sin they covered themselves with garments made out of fig leaves. Fig leaves! Have you ever tried to make anything out of fig leaves? Fig leaves are not big and I imagine they would make clothes which would not survive the elements for too long. Apparently, the sap in fig leaves can cause a skin rash and this would make wearing them very uncomfortable! Our Father stoops once more and makes them garments made from animal skins. I imagine him seeing them and feeling pity for their half-baked attempt at clothing themselves. I can almost hear the cry of his heart, "My children deserve better than that!"

As man wanders off on his journey of independence God does not change. Isaiah 9:6 tells us that God is the Everlasting Father. Man's choice of independence did not stop God being a Father. He has always been Father and always will be. Nothing we can do will ever change that. Nothing we can do will ever stop God being Love. We cannot change who he is.

A father does not stop being a father because his kids rebel. A father is a father forever. Human fathers, of course, are not perfect and their love can be, or seem to be, conditional. But the Father's love is never conditional. God does not stop revealing his heart to his children. He tries to woo them back. He provides for them century after century and he leads them and guides them. He protects them. He does everything he can to end their journey of independence. The one thing he does not do is force an end to the rebellion; as we have seen that would not be love. He seeks to do everything he can to ignite the spark of love within his people's hearts in order to turn them round. But the rebellion continues.

Throughout the whole of the Old Testament there is a cry from our Father's heart as he seeks to win his children back.

> For the LORD has spoken: "I reared children and brought them up, but they have rebelled against me." (Isaiah 1:2)

> I myself said, "How gladly would I treat you like sons and give you a desirable land, the most beautiful inheritance of any nation. I thought you would call me 'Father' and not turn away from following me." (Jeremiah 3:19)

Ultimately he revealed himself to us in the person of Jesus who became the way for us to come back to the Father. Throughout the Old Testament

God was known by many names. Each one highlighted one of his many attributes. But when Jesus came he revealed who God was - Father! Jesus summed up the nature, character and personality of God in one word. He was the only one who knew God that intimately and he came to reveal the truth about him. The Father was Jesus' Father and he is our Father too. Jesus not only taught us this but he lived out the relationship of being a son, both to Joseph and Mary and to God. As we shall see later that sonship defined Jesus not only in what he did but in who he was.

Jesus showed us that God is Father. As we know, it was not just the formal title "father" but it was the intimate, relaxed and conversational "Abba" or "Daddy". His death made it possible for us once again to be brought back into that intimate relationship with God where we, too, can call him "Daddy" or "Papa".

John 14:18 records Jesus saying "I will not leave you as orphans" – a verse we will explore in more detail later. This verse is followed by a promise that our hearts can become the Father's home (John 17:23). The Father went to great lengths to show us that his essential nature has not changed. He is the Eternal Father.

So what is this Father like?

When Moses asked God what he was like, he was taken up Mount Sinai to find the answer. As God's presence came down in a cloud, passing in front of Moses, he spoke and revealed his nature:

> *Then the* LORD *came down in the cloud and stood there with him and proclaimed his name, the* LORD. *And he passed in front of Moses, proclaiming, "The* LORD, *the* LORD, *the compassionate and gracious God, slow to anger, abounding in love and faithfulness, maintaining love to thousands, and forgiving wickedness, rebellion and sin. Yet he does not leave the guilty unpunished; he punishes the children and their children for the sin of the fathers to the third and fourth generation." (Exodus 34:6-7)*

Too often we dwell on the last part of these verses. We think of God as judgemental, continually looking out for our sin and then jumping on us to deal with all our imperfections. Maybe we live in fear of his wrath catching up with us and hurling us into outer darkness forever. There will be a judgement day and those who have never come to him for forgiveness will be separated from him forever. But now is the season of grace. Now is the time when we can see him as he is and be the recipients of his love and favour.

God is compassionate and loving. He is gracious and slow to become angry. He stands with his arms open wide, ready to receive his children and to shower us with love and blessings. He is not distant and angry; his heart is to forgive and to receive us.

Jesus is the exact representation of God. To see what the Father is like we can look at the life of Jesus. He met people in their place of need. When they were sick, he healed them. When the wine ran out at the wedding, he provided generously. When the hurting needed comfort, he comforted them. So it is with the Father. He meets us in our place of need and appeals to our hearts in order to satisfy our deepest longings. He does not deal only with the superficial issues but he is interested in the very core of our being.

The Father's desire is that we are transformed into Jesus' likeness. As we walk with him so we become like his son, Jesus. This is not a burden; it is a relationship. We have the same access to the Father as Jesus had and so we can come to him in our own right and talk to him as a son or daughter talks to their father.

God does not compel us to love him. He can't do that as it would go against his very nature. All he does is love us and as he does, love is drawn out of us. He does not demand obedience but as we love him we start to obey him. It is a natural progression; obedience is not required of us but it flows as we respond to God with our love. We can only love him because he first loved us. Trying to please God can lead us into legalism and religion but responding to him out of love is freedom. His invitation to us is to walk freely as his sons and daughters.

God really is our Father. He knows everything about us. He chose the day we would be born and the places we would live. He knit us together in our mother's womb. He is the Father of our spirit. We were conceived in his heart before the beginning of time. Not one of us is a mistake.

God has always been Father and he always will be Father. His heart's desire is to be a Father to you!

Notes:
1. By Bob Merrill - 1961

Chapter 2

Redeeming the Orphan Heart

"I will not leave you as orphans"
John 14:18

God has a plan. In fact, it is much more than a plan. It is his heart's desire.

When God created the world and everything in it, he did it for a purpose. He was not bored nor was he lonely. He certainly did not need to find something to occupy his time! The Trinity was complete in itself but the love and unity enjoyed by Father, Son and Spirit was to be shared with a family. Knowing it would all go wrong might be enough to stop us having such a plan - but not God! He wanted a family and he wants a bride for his son.

God's original intention was that he would enjoy us and that we would enjoy him forever. When we read the Bible without any filters or preconceived ideas it is truly amazing what he says about us.

> *"You are worthy, O Lord our God, to receive glory and honour and power. For you created everything, and it is for your pleasure that they exist and were created." (Rev 4:11 NLT)*

"... everyone who is called by name, whom I created for my glory, whom I formed and made." (Isaiah 43:7)

"... all things were created by him and for him." Colossians 1:16

He made each one of us to bring him pleasure. All too often we believe that the "everything" in Revelation 4:11 excludes us! We picture God taking great delight in the creation of the natural world but it seems the creation of man has brought him nothing but trouble. We imagine him enjoying looking at the mountains and the forests or the seas and the lakes but frowning with contempt as he looks upon us. We see him enjoying the earth's expanse but waving a stick of judgement over mankind.

Although everything was created to give God pleasure, sadly the fallen world and the fallen nature of humanity means that there are many things that sadden his heart. He delights in us glorifying him and bringing him pleasure. As we are awakened by his love we become aware of the glory resting on us and we can enter into the glorious inheritance which he has for his children.

When God says he wants **everything** to bring him pleasure he means everything! Even us! We were made to bring God pleasure; he actually enjoys our company. He enjoys being with us and being involved in our daily lives. There is nothing that is too small or insignificant for him to be interested in. Colossians 1:16 tells us that **all** things were made by him and **for** him.

My wife and I really enjoy having our family with us. The girls are away from home most of the time now but it is a great delight when they come back and visit. When all six of us are together it is wonderful to see the four children chatting and catching up on their news. It give us great pleasure to sit back and watch the family interacting together. How much more is that pleasure magnified for God when he can enjoy the companionship and friendship of his children. It satisfies his heart to have his family around him.

No-one is excluded from this. There are no second class citizens in the Kingdom of Heaven. All of us can come to the Father and know that he accepts us, loves us and welcomes us into his family. You may feel that the Father could not love you or that the wrong things you have done are too bad to let you come into his presence. His love bridges that gap and you are welcome. He wants to make a home in your heart just as much as he wants to make a home with the next person. There is nothing that you can do or have done that takes you outside his love. YOU were made for his pleasure. YOU were made to bring him glory.

Not only do we bring him pleasure, but we are made to be like his son, Jesus. In Romans 8:28-29 we read that those called by God are predestined to become like Jesus. This means the Father always had it in mind that we would be like Jesus - not cardboard cut-outs, but like him in character and in love. God has not inserted a computer chip in us and programmed us to be an exact replica, where we all have the same personality and are unable to think for ourselves. He has created each of us to be completely unique with a wonderful individual personality. Being like Jesus means having a heart like his - being a son or daughter to the Father and loving him with all our heart, soul and mind. Becoming like Jesus is not something we attain through hard work but is a gift, given to us through the grace of Jesus. Remember, we can only love because he first loved us. Being like Jesus is a response to the Father's love in our heart.

Although the Trinity was complete in itself, God's plan was that we would share in that completeness and unity. In John 17 Jesus prays that the love the Father has for him will also be in us. As Jesus always prayed in accordance with his Father's will, we can have confidence that this prayer will be answered. We are loved in the same way and with the same love as he loves Jesus. Wow! The beauty and intimacy of the relationship enjoyed before the beginning of time is our inheritance. This is what we were made for.

God takes great delight in all of his children. None are excluded from his love; we were all made to bring him pleasure.

As we read Genesis 1 we see the power of God's spoken word: "Let there be..." and there was! As the Father spoke creative words, so the Son brought it all into being. But on the sixth day God did more than issue a simple command. Instead he said, "Let us make man in our image". "Let us" – this was a work that involved all three persons of the Godhead. God stepped down to the created earth and started to do something very strange.

He gathered dust into a pile and began to make it into a shape.

I have made sandcastles on the beach (not one of my favourite activities) and you do need to have the right type of sand. It has to be damp enough but not too wet. It has to be pressed into the bucket but not too tightly. Sandcastles are a challenge for any father.

But here the Father makes something out of dust. He shaped it until he was satisfied with its form. Then he breathed life into it. The Message captures this moment: *"God formed man out of dirt from the ground and blew into his nostrils the breath of life. The man came alive – a living soul"* (Genesis 2:7 The Message). The breath of life came straight from the Father which would have been a very intimate moment. His life came into us and gave us life. We became his children.

This was the start of the human race - created to bring pleasure to the Father, made in the image and likeness of Jesus and carrying the spirit of God breathed into us so intimately.

But it all went wrong, badly wrong.

There is an enemy who sought to destroy God's plan and ruin the beautiful creation made by a loving Father. Revelation 12:7 tells of the battle which was waged in Heaven. Michael, the great warrior angel, fought against Satan and his rebellious angels. Satan was not strong enough and he lost his place in Heaven. He was hurled to the earth and ever since has been bent on leading the whole world astray.

Satan set himself against God. He did not just want to be like him; he wanted to *be* God. He wanted God's place for himself. In Isaiah 14 his desire is summarised in five "I wills".

> *"I will ascend to Heaven.*
> *I will raise my throne above God's.*
> *I will sit enthroned on the mount of the assembly.*
> *I will ascend to the top of the clouds.*
> *I will make myself like the Most High".*
> *(verses 13-14)*

Satan was not after equality with God; he was after supremacy in creation. He failed. He was hurled from the presence of God. For all eternity he stepped out of God's Fatherhood and love. Never again will he regain his position as one of the mighty angels of the Lord of Hosts. He was thrown out with force.

Well, we know how the story continues, with the tempting of the woman (with Adam right by her side), the desire for independence and the succumbing to the lies of the serpent. In the picture of two broken people being banished from the Father's presence, we see a total separation from love. The empty orphan heart descended on them and through them upon the whole human race. All the comfort and nurture they had known was now lost!

After Cain had killed his brother, he was sent to wander the earth restlessly. How empty his heart must have felt. That same emptiness has settled on each of our hearts as we, too, have moved outside of God's perfect plan. Until our hearts come home to the Father, there is a real sense of us wandering through life restlessly. We know there is a void inside us that yearns for something more. We know it was not meant to be this way but somehow the truth eludes us. We cannot find what we are looking for. We have all taken on the fallen nature of man and stepped out of God's care and love.

But there is a promise.

The Old Testament ends with a glimpse of a brighter day - a day when the hearts of the children will, once more, be turned back to the heart of the Father. There is hope.

And then Jesus breaks into the scene. He comes from the Father to become the way for us to return home to the Father. He comes to bring light and life into a dark world. He calls time on Satan's activity and his apparent rule and reign. He comes once and for all to destroy the works of the evil one and makes it possible for us to enjoy relationship with the Father once again.

In the previous chapter we saw how Adam and Eve's banishment from the garden was an act of love. It prevented them from eating of the tree of life and living in eternal separation from God. Jesus shows us another extreme act of love. He took all our sin and hung on a rough wooden cross. He suffered the most horrific death of the day and, worst of all, he felt totally separated from his Father. But that act of love put an end to our fallen state. As the curtain in the temple was torn in two, so God broke out of the temple and started to live in the hearts of men and women. This had always been his plan. He had always wanted to live in people's hearts; he had never wanted to be stuck in a temple! Jesus died on the cross so the Father's love could be released into our hearts. Once again he can come and make our hearts his home.

God is the Eternal Father. His plan has never changed; he does not have a plan 'B'. His plan was to live in relationship and friendship with his children. He knew that we would make wrong choices and he could have prevented them but, as we have seen, that would have gone against his nature. We were objects of his wrath (Ephesians 2:3-4), but now we have been made alive in Christ. We were lost but now have been found.

In John 14:18 Jesus says we will not be left as orphans. In some ways this verse seems out of context because Jesus is talking about his death and the coming of the Holy Spirit. But Jesus knows that through his death a way will be made for us to come back into relationship with the Father. He knows that the veil separating us from God will be torn in two and that once more his home can be in our hearts. Jesus knows that the Holy Spirit is a spirit of sonship which enables us to cry "Abba, Father". He can see that the end of our orphan ways is at hand and that the emptiness of our hearts is about to change in order that we will, once again, be filled with the Father's love. He is able to say, on behalf of his Father, "I will not leave you as orphans, I will come to you". Jesus came in order that our orphan heart could be redeemed.

His plan is still to live in friendship and relationship with his children. Nothing has changed. God is determined to carry out his plan, not through force but in love, perfect love. He has made a way for us to come back to him, not through our own effort but through the sacrifice of his son. Despite our short comings he still takes great pleasure in us. He delights in you!

Chapter 3

Our Journey To Love

Our lives are a journey.

In fact there are two journeys which have become so mixed up that we no longer know which is the real one.

Much of our time and energy is spent on our day to day living. We are caught up in what we do and what we are trying to achieve or want to become. We want to do a good job at work, even if that only means showing up regularly and being on time. We want to look good both in terms of our outward appearance and the things we accomplish. We want to be noticed and to be thought well off. We like other people's good opinions and their approval. It becomes important to us that our act looks as if it is all together. (But remember it is only an act!)

This is the external journey. The one which everyone sees - those in our families, our workplaces and even in the church. People are always watching and waiting to see what we are really like. They watch and monitor our targets and our performance. They want to see how we cope with pressure and, often, how we compare with them. Because this journey is so public we may start to believe that it is the most important journey we are on. Before long it may take over and become all consuming.

This journey asks the question: "Who am I?"

Then, there is the second journey which is far more important than the external one but is not so clearly seen or understood. This is the internal journey of our hearts. It is where the real **me** is. It is where my struggles and successes are really found. It is the place where I can start to hear the voice of One calling me into an intimate relationship. This journey is hidden but it defines us in a much more real way than the external journey of our day to day lives. It is this journey that shapes who we are and where we are really going. It is this journey that has so much more meaning and value than the external one.

Like the first journey this too asks the question: "Who am I?"

Each journey asks the same question but the answer can be very different. The answer about the external journey will not satisfy the deep longings of our hearts. Achieving all the right goals and targets will never make us hit the ultimate mark as there will always be another level to conquer. Like climbing a mountain there is always another peak over the horizon. As soon as we achieve others' expectations they move the goal-posts to heap more on to us. Satisfaction is only temporary! We may be satisfied for a moment but it drains away leaving us searching once again.

The deepest longings of our hearts are only satisfied when we find what we are made for.

We are all searching for love. Our problem is not so much that we are searching but where we are looking to find the answer. There are many counterfeits which clamour for our attention and our time. They try to seduce us with the lure of easy pickings and quick gratification. They do not satisfy for any length of time and leave us wanting to come back for more. Counterfeit lovers are short term and need constant feeding!

For men, jobs, sport, sex, alcohol or even church can become counterfeit lovers. Our work can become a god with the pursuit of another's affirmation and pleasure. It can become a place where there is fulfilment or even escapism from the daily, and often boring, routine of family life. A job can give us our identity – it can define who we are, give us security and a sense of well being. But the pleasure is short-lived until another set of monthly targets disperses whatever achievement we may have gained. Women can be lured by the short-term lovers of clothing, fashion or food. These too, provide short -term comfort but they can never satisfy the deep longings. Such pleasure is short-lived and as fashions change the dissatisfied move on.

We can waste hours, if not years, pursuing this external journey and all the while becoming more frustrated by the lack of any lasting sense of meaning to life. That sense of well-being keeps eluding us.

But there is a place we can come to where the deep longings of our hearts can be satisfied. In fact, it is not a place but a person. That person is God the Father. 1 John 4:16 tells us that God is love. Love is not just one of his many attributes. It is who he is. It is the core of his very being. The complete expression of love is found in a person. He is not another substitute or counterfeit, nor another short term lover. He is the real thing! Everything that God does, he does out of love and for love.

The love of the Father banishes fear. How often do you worry about the future? Is God in your plans and desires? Perfect love casts out fear so with him all the apprehensions about the future can be taken care of. It was because of God's love for us that he sent his only son, Jesus, to *"clear away our sins and the damage they've done to our relationship with God"* (1 John 4:10 The Message). It is only this perfect love that can answer the question "Who am I?" as we shall see in a moment.

God demonstrates his love in many ways. The greatest of all was by sending Jesus to win us back to him and to claim our hearts as his own once again. There are many other ways in which his love is shown and which are all freely available to us.

Here are some: he is mighty to save, he delights in us, he rejoices over us with singing (Zephaniah 3:17). He cares for us like a shepherd cares for his sheep (Isaiah 40:11). He comes to us and wipes the tears away from our eyes (Revelation 21:3-4). He is close to the broken hearted (Psalm 34:18). He created us in our mother's womb (Psalm 139:13). He encourages us (2 Thessalonians 2:16). He thinks about us (Psalm 139:17). This is not an exhaustive list but merely some of the practical ways God shows his love to us. These are not theoretical possibilities but they are real day to day expressions of his love. Next time you go through some heartache, why not take a moment to ask him to come and wipe away your tears! When you struggle with rejection or fear ask him to express his care for you like a shepherd cares for his flock. Ask him, either on your own or with some close friends. You will not be disappointed because he delights to shower his love on his children.

This is not rocket science. This seems simple and it is! But sometimes our pride can stop us coming with the simple childlike faith that Jesus talks about. God's love is not attained through a formula or by us earning it. It is available simply because God is love.

We all need love. Ideally, it should be the very foundation of our lives. But in our journey through life many of us do not receive the love we need. Our mothers and fathers should have given us a foundation of love but in a fallen world even the best human parents fail to give their children the quality of love which God intended us to have. When the foundation is lacking we often turn elsewhere to try and find what we do not have.

The need for love leads us to seek affirmation in all sorts of places and with all sorts of people. It is a search for value and acceptance. We need to know that someone wants us, even if for the wrong reasons. All of this leaves us empty, with the fundamental cry of our hearts unanswered.

The truth is that we have all been loved with an everlasting love (Jeremiah 31:3). God draws us to himself with his love and his kindness. His love is unconditional. It is his love that will make us totally safe as we become hidden in him (Psalm 32:7). He becomes our light and salvation and we need have no fear (Psalm 27:1). God has a perfect plan for us, a good plan that is for our prosperity, not to harm us but to give us hope and a future (Jeremiah 29:11).

It is the satisfaction of our deepest desire for love that we are all searching for. We may not be aware of it but this is our greatest need. The answer to the question "who am I?" is found as we become immersed in love. Our real identity is not in what we do for a living or how high we climb up the social ladder. Our real identity is found when we know that we are loved by Father God. Value is found in being known by another. When we are really known we feel affirmed and the loneliness and isolation we live in can start to disperse.

We cannot strive to earn this love. It is a complete gift of grace. To begin the internal journey of the heart we have to let go of the 'oughts' and the 'duty' that weigh us down. We don't experience God's love by keeping rules or becoming involved in religious programmes but by developing a relationship with him. Relationships are not prescribed by rules or structure - they are a flow of life! The external journey is self-centred whereas the internal journey is centred around the Person who is love.

Let me end this chapter with a well known verse:

"How great is the love that the
Father has lavished on us, that
we should be called children of
God! And that is what we are! (1
John 3:1).

The Father does not hold anything back as he
lavishes his love on you and me. He calls us his
children. The journey of your heart is all about
finding the One who loves you so much that he
lavishes perfect love on you all the time. This is
extravagance beyond measure!

Before you read on take a few moments to
consider which journey you are pursuing. If you
know that you are pursuing the external journey
ask yourself "Am I really satisfied?"

Be honest. Then take a few more moments to ask
Father God to lavish his love on you.

Chapter 4

I Will Be A Father To YOU

"I will be a Father to you and you will be my sons and daughters"
2 Corinthians 6:18

Think for a moment what it must have been like for Adam and his wife, created as adults living in perfect love and enjoying a friendship with their Creator and their Father. They lacked nothing; they were totally dependent on God and looked to him to supply all their needs. There was a simplicity of relationship which, as we know, was lost. The joy is, it is ours to regain.

As we grow up in a fallen world we start to build walls around our hearts. We are hurt by our families, our schools and our work places and so we try to protect ourselves against more hurt and pain. We have our own way of behaving in order to stay safe. We learn the social etiquette that enables us to put on a brave face but which does not allow us to share our heart. We develop gifts and abilities which lead to us doing our own thing and becoming independent.

Growing up produces a greater independence and some of that is right. However, as we grow as Christians, the Father's desire for us is not independence but a greater dependence on him.

God is faithful and he does not give up on us. His desire is that we live in relationship with him and particularly that we know he is a Father to us.

Throughout the Old Testament, there is a cry that comes from the Father's heart which was verbalised by Jesus in John 14:18: *"I will not leave you as orphans, I will come to you"*. God did not want to leave us in that state of separation for he simply could not leave us fatherless. He wanted to restore everything that had been snatched away through the fall, so he constantly sought to draw his people back to him. What he really wanted was to live in their hearts and, to God, this was more important than their sacrifices.

We gain many glimpses of the Father's heart as he seeks to embrace his children again. The Psalms are full of tender promises of his love and care. He even declares that he will be a Father to the fatherless (Psalm 68:5). The great prophet Isaiah begins with a declaration from the heart of God that it was he who had reared the Israelites as children and brought them up, only for them to rebel against him (Isaiah 1:2).

There are two small words which have completely changed my understanding of God and the way I relate to him. They are very ordinary words that we use a thousand times a day! They are the words "to you" in 2 Corinthians 6:18 – "I will be a Father **to you**". This verse can bring the theology of God's Father heart right into our hearts. It can make all our concepts and theories very personal. It can change our view and knowledge of God to become an impartation of life.

God's love needs to become immensely personal. Although he is Father of creation and Father of mankind he is not distant or afar off. He is not too busy running the universe to be concerned with you. He is interested in a personal and intimate relationship with you.

This revelation is for everyone. Too often I hear people say they don't see the relevance of the Father-heart message to them. They tell me they had good parents who cared and provided for them, who made sure they were secure and well grounded. Such families are a wonderful blessing and a tremendous inheritance. But the implication that the Father's love is only for the hurting or broken-hearted misses the point completely. Nowhere in Scripture does it say that God only reveals his heart to those we call the hurting or broken. What it does say is that those with a childlike heart can understand the mysteries of the kingdom. The truth is that all of us have areas of our lives that need healing and restoration, where we need the Father's love to come and fill us. We may try to hide them or be reluctant to wear our hearts on our sleeve, but all of us have such wounds.

Even the most perfect man who ever lived needed to know that his Father loved him. On two specific occasions God spoke words of affirmation out loud to his son, Jesus. It cannot be right that we set ourselves apart from his love when it was the very source of life to Jesus.

It takes humility to receive God's love. Many of us have been taught to have everything all together and present a polished act for all to see. Well, let's remember that it is only an act. Let's give up the act for the real thing.

There are hindrances that prevent us receiving this personal fathering which we will look at in a later chapter, but first I want to address a few misconceptions about God's nature as a Father.

Fathering is not a single sexual or physical act. I remember a pastor telling me once about a man in his town. It was this man's goal to 'father' as many children as possible. He was not interested in love or commitment and he certainly did not care about the girls who became his prey. All he wanted was another 'trophy' on his shelf! Once the girl had conceived he would walk away to begin the search for his next innocent and unsuspecting victim. He had 'fathered' many children but was not prepared to be a father to them in a loving relationship of care, security and provision. If that is how you were conceived, let me tell you as gently as I can, that God knows all about you, values you highly and wants to provide all the comfort, security and love you need. He planned you before the beginning of time. He formed you in your mother's womb and he chose the day you would be born and the place that you would live. He loves you very much.

Secondly, experiencing an absentee father can also distort our understanding of God as Father. Divorce rates are high. Between one third and one half of marriages in the UK end in divorce and the frightening thing is that the divorce rates are not much lower in the church than in society as a whole. Many children grow up in families where there is no father or where they only see him at weekends or holidays. They have little reference for what a father should be like and superimpose that limited view on God. Fathers can also be absent through untimely death. I have many good memories of my own father. He cared for us all, worked hard to provide for us and we had some wonderful holidays. But he was taken from us when I was ten. In Africa where disease is so prevalent there are many fathers who don't live to see their children. Also, some fathers are sadly absent even when they are present! They hide in the office, behind a newspaper, computer or in front of the TV. They are there but they are not available.

A third way our view of God as Father is shaped is by a belief that fatherhood means domination, anger or control. If our own fathers have been controlling or angry we may project that image on to God. Domination and manipulation cause us to hide our hearts away to protect them from further hurt. We push down painful feelings because we don't want to be crushed. If all we have experienced from our fathers is a crushing of the spirit, we close down to anyone who looks like a father figure.

It is not only an experience of poor or abusive fathering which can shape our view of God and therefore affect the way we relate to him. Having a good father can also be a hindrance as that, too, has its limitations. If your father was good how much better do you think God is? On a scale of 0 - 100 if God scores 100 then there is probably not a great deal of difference between a 'good' father and a 'bad' father. Both will be near the bottom of the score sheet.

The good news is that God is not limited to our experiences. He is the perfect and eternal Father. He is not absent or controlling. He is not manipulative or angry towards us. His desire is that we come to him as his children and allow him to father us in a very personal and intimate way. He can change our love deficits into love surpluses. All the love that we have been robbed of can be supplied by him. He can mend our hearts and then fill them with his love.

This is not a one-off experience but a way of life. True fathering is a lifelong process. God is a Father who *wants* to be involved in our lives. His fatherhood is active and ongoing. He does not leave us to muddle on in our own strength but calls us into the shelter of his wings where he can protect us, care for us and nurture us. And he wants to have fun along the way. God is actually more fun-loving than anyone. From some of the things that happen we can see he must have a tremendous sense of humour! In his book "Letters to Malcolm" C S Lewis writes: "Joy is the serious business of Heaven". Sadly, joy is not something Christians are particularly known for, though the Bible frequently mentions joy. If the joy of the Lord filled us we would become a more attractive group of people!

In the church today there are many spiritual orphans - people who know their sins are forgiven but constantly try to earn God's favour through their own effort. They are trying to make their own way in life and make a name for themselves. God is our Father and he does not want us to live like orphans. He wants a family. He wants sons and daughters. He wants us to stop striving and come to a place of rest in him, knowing that his favour is on us.

Orphan hearts find it hard to believe that they are loved. God wants us to know that we are loved, as Jesus knew that he was loved. If living in love was good enough for Jesus then it must be good enough for us.

I have written a good deal about the Father's love bringing healing and wholeness to broken hearts, for it is true. He loves to come to us and heal hearts that have been damaged. He loves to scoop us up and fill the love deficit in our lives. The restoration and renewal of our hearts may not take place in an instant but is often a process where layers of pain are gradually removed over time. It is wonderful that there is healing for broken and rejected hearts but God has a bigger plan for each us. The restoration of our hearts and a life lived in love are not separate things but are inextricably bound together. He does not simply heal us and then leave us alone. He wants us to enjoy a relationship with him where we learn to know and rely on his love (1 John 4:16). These are experiential words and describe a way of living for us that can model the life Jesus lived.

You may be familiar with 2 Corinthians 3:18: *"And we, who with unveiled faces all reflect the Lord's glory, are being transformed into his likeness"*. What does this mean? Hebrews 2:10

tells us that God is bringing many sons to glory. It is possible to be caught up with what God is *doing* rather than who he is. Many people are happy to come to God for what he can do for them or for what he can give them. But having received that gift their lives are not substantially changed. Of course, God wants to do things for us and he has many good gifts to give us but he wants us to go beyond merely understanding his deeds. He wants to us to know who he is and to be changed into his likeness. Moses was a man who knew God's *ways,* whereas the people of Israel knew only his *deeds* (Psalm 103:7). The healing of our hearts can be the doorway by which we allow the transforming power of grace to work in us, so that we begin to experience the freedom which is promised to us and, like Moses, start to know his ways.

So, the Father's love is not an optional extra. It is not just for the 'broken hearted'. It is for all of us. It is for all those who desire to live in freedom and to enjoy the glorious transformation of becoming more like Jesus. We will explore more fully what it means to share the glory of Jesus and to live in freedom in chapters 10 and 11.

A year or so after I started my website *afathertoyou.com* I felt God lead me back to 2 Corinthians 6. In verses 13 and 17 Paul encourages the Corinthians to open their hearts to him, to come out from the ways of the world and allow God to be a Father to them. What a wonderful opportunity! Come out from the ways of the world, allow your heart to be open and let God be a Father to you.

God does not want us to live a narrow existence. He wants us to come out into a spacious place where we are free from restriction (Job 36:16) and where he can be a Father to us.

Let me come back to my two small words – "to you". This promise is for everyone. In one sense what our earthly father (or mother) was like is irrelevant. We all need to know the gentle, kind and overwhelming love of Father God. All of us can enjoy the freedom that is promised to his children. We can become rooted and grounded in his love. It is not an optional extra. It is for you! God really, really wants to be a Father to you – personally, today and forever – **to you!**

Chapter 5

Hindrances to Knowing God as Father

It would be easy to read this chapter as a list of things which we should not do. If we do them we feel condemned and if we don't we could end up trying to tick all the right boxes and in some way try to earn a relationship with God. However, these are real hindrances which I need to highlight. At the end of the chapter I will try to give some simple keys to breaking through. Books have been written on each of the hindrances I am going to mention and I am therefore going to be brief as I do not want them to be stumbling blocks as you come to know God as Father. We may struggle with some of them but they do not need to consume us.

Hindrances arising from relationships with parents

Some of the main hindrances to us knowing God as Father arise from our relationships with our natural fathers. The next few pages contain some huge generalisations but you may see things you recognise and areas in your heart that Father wants to heal.

Performance Oriented Fathers
Fathers who are performance oriented place harsh demands on their children for perfection and obedience. Often they do so without meaning

to and would be horrified if they were told this was a characteristic in their life! It is almost as if straight A's are not good enough. Performance oriented fathers criticise their children for getting 90%. "Is that the best you could do?" may be their response. Their love appears to be expressed only when the target is hit, and then the target moves to a higher level.

Such love is conditional and children feel shame when they fail. This type of fathering can leave us thinking God is demanding and that his love always has strings attached. We feel the shame of not being good enough.

Passive Fathers
Passive fathers place no great demands on their children. They do not demonstrate love or affection. They leave children to do their own thing and work on the basis that everything is alright unless they are told otherwise. Western fathers often fall into this category (another sweeping generalisation). They are good providers but have a very low level of involvement with their children. They are physically present but emotionally absent.

Passive fathering leaves us with a view of God being uninvolved in our lives. He seems to leave us to work things out for ourselves. This may cause us to develop an independent spirit, to make frantic efforts to catch God's attention, or to accept with resignation that an intimate, personal relationship with God is not possible for us.

Absentee Fathers

Absentee fathers are no longer present in the home because of death, divorce, work or abandonment. More and more children are growing up without a father in the home. It is not uncommon for children to take upon themselves the blame for a separation or divorce. They blame themselves that their parents could not get on and withdraw into a life of shame and loneliness. Where a father is a workaholic, children often feel it is because of them that Dad does not want to come home in the evening or at weekends. Children take on the blame and live in shame.

If we have been abandoned by our earthly father, why shouldn't God abandon us? And so we grow up believing in a God who may abandon us and leave us as orphans. We settle for a life of striving and making our own way without the help of anyone else.

Authoritarian Fathers

Authoritarian fathers are more interested in the law than in love. They are stern and demand unquestioning obedience. They need to be right. In fact, this is more important to them than having relationship. They rule their children with fear and intimidation. No opinion other than theirs can be tolerated. Many do so with all the right motives and often such sternness reflects their own upbringing.

Fathering like this may make us see God as legalistic and demanding, and cause us to give him our obedience out of fear rather than love and relationship.

Abusive Fathers
Abuse comes in many forms and I hesitate to mention them for the fear which may rise in your heart. The very mention may make your stomach feel knotted and sick. But I do so because I know that God can heal and take away the effects of serious abuse. Verbal, physical, emotional or sexual abuse – especially by someone who was supposed to represent love and care - steals something precious from us and trust is betrayed to an horrific extent. Abuse leads to anger and fear. Hearts are locked up and emotions deadened. All too often it is the abused (as well as the abuser) who feels extreme guilt and shame.

If our natural father has abused us, then God may appear untrustworthy. We may be angry at him and unable to enjoy the intimacy that he offers.

Good Fathers
Why am I mentioning a good father as a hindrance to knowing God as Father?

Surely this is the ideal, what all fathers should be - a model of our Heavenly Father. Yet I have spoken to many people who have had good fathers but struggle with God being a Father to them. Indeed, I have actually known the fathers in several cases and they were good fathers! A good human father can set a ceiling which limits our expectations. Having experienced a good father, we wonder what can be better and so our own experience satisfies us and we are content to settle there.

Do not let a good father, with all his love, care and encouragement stop you from finding the perfect Father. A good human father is no substitute for the love of your Heavenly Father.

Some Other Hindrances

Let me mention some other hindrances which prevent us from finding the perfect Father. What may be a hindrance for one will not be a problem for someone else. These things can grip us but they do not need to control us. As you read, ask the Father to show you areas of your heart that need adjustment. Remember this chapter is not here to condemn you but to help you find freedom.

Hidden Sin

Our sin was dealt with once and for all at the cross. The cause of our separation from God has been removed. But hidden sin can grip us and hold us in guilt and shame. Remember how Adam and his wife felt great shame and tried to avoid exposing their sin. They could not come back to God and let him deal with it. They tried to deal with it their own way and failed. 1 John 1:9 assures us that if we confess our sin he *will* forgive us. We are encouraged to walk in the light with one another and with God (1 John 1:7 and Ephesians 5:8-10). Hidden sin keeps us locked up. When we walk in the light we have intimate fellowship with the Father (1 John 1:3,6).

Legalism

Legalism is trying to earn God's favour by keeping rules. Our own righteousness is like filthy rags and leads to us becoming independent rather than dependent on him. In the end, legalism leads to self-righteousness or despair. Either way, it hinders the flow of Father's unconditional love in our lives. The Father's love is a message of grace and there is no way we can do anything that will make God love us anymore. If we feel more righteous he does not love us any more. If we live under a cloud of guilt we are no less loved!

Fear of Rejection

Fear leads to mistrust and mistrust leads to unhealthy relationships. Fear paralyses but love releases. Psalm 27:10 tells us that even if our mother and father forsake us God will receive us. Abandonment is a great snare to the hearts of God's children. It is a lie planted in our heart that we do not matter, that we are not wanted and that our life is of no value. All lies are spoken by the enemy, not by the lover of our hearts. His love is high enough, deep enough, wide enough and long enough to make sure that no-one can escape it (Ephesians 3:14-19).

Pride

God resists the proud (James 4:6). Pride is our vain attempt at being self sufficient and trying to live a life without God. You can have a go but it is very hard work! Jesus was totally dependent on his Father for everything. If living a dependent life was good enough for Jesus it is surely good enough for us.

Unbelief

Jesus said some startling things about people and their unbelief. He had lived among the people around him and revealed the true nature of his Father, yet still many could not believe. Our limited understanding can stop us believing the truth – the truth that we are limited! Jesus asks us to have a childlike faith because that will cause mountains to be cast into the sea. Hebrews 11:6 tells us that without faith it is not possible to please God!

Shame

Shame comes on us in many different ways and causes us to hide from God. We try to cover ourselves and look good before our parents, our peers or our friends, even before our pastors. It can cause us to promote ourselves and pull others down in an attempt to find acceptance. The truth is that God accepts us as we are. Instead of shame he gives us a double blessing (Isaiah 61:7). If we trust him we will not be put to shame (Romans 10:11).

Rejecting the Parents God Gave Us

Jesus was always a true son in his heart. This is something we will explore more fully in a later chapter. He was a son to Joseph and Mary, to a spiritual father (son of David) and of course to God. If we have a right relationship with our own parents it is easier to walk with God as a Father. As we honour our parents so we come under a blessing.

Deception
The thief comes to kill, steal and destroy (John 10:10). Jesus came that we might have life in all its fullness. Satan is constantly lying about the true nature of God because the last thing he wants is for us to discover what God is really like. He wants us to believe that God is distant, angry and harsh and that he demands obedience and service at all costs. The truth sets us free (John 8:32).

Unforgiveness
"Bitterness is a poison pill we swallow, thinking it will kill someone else" (Jack Winter). Unforgiveness keeps us in a prison. As we release those who have offended us and ask God for compassion towards them, we can walk into freedom. Cancelling the debt they owe us and releasing them from the wrong they have done, opens the way for us walk into a wide open space. Forgiveness is such an important key to enable us to receive the Father's love that we will consider it in detail in the next chapter.

*****

At the start of this chapter I said I would try to provide some keys to dealing with these hindrances. Despite being hindrances they should not consume us and keep us from knowing God as Father. The power of grace and the redeeming work of the cross are far more powerful than any of these things that can bind us temporarily.

Whatever our experience so far we can ask and expect God to father us. Too often we know the theology that God is 'Father' but do not enter into the reality of him being a Father **to** us. There is a huge difference between the theory and the relational experience.

Occasionally I receive an email from someone who has visited my website. What they have read has helped them and maybe brought a revelation or an understanding to their hearts. But their question often is 'How does God become a Father to me?'. They tell me there are no conferences they can go to and no supportive church in their locality. They feel they are reaching out on their own for something they are not sure they can grasp. I write back and encourage them to ask God to reveal himself to them. He has promised to be a Father to us and that is not dependent on any conference or other event. It depends solely on the truth of his word and his love for us.

Sometimes it is good to take time out to seek God, to listen to CDs or download messages from the internet about the Father's love. But the important thing is to ask in faith. God wants to be a Father to us. He has promised that he will and it is his greatest delight to draw us into relationship with him. Do you remember the seed of faith you had when you became a Christian? If you were like me it was only a small seed and a small step of obedience that brought about a changed life and heart. Receiving his love requires the same small step. His love is not hidden but is available to anyone who will ask.

One of the main ways we can leave these hindrances behind is to reach the end of ourselves and have a cry in our hearts that says "God I need you to do something, I need you to change my heart". Asking God to be your Father is a prayer which he loves to answer.

Earlier I mentioned hidden sin. God does not turn his face away from sin. In the garden he pursued Adam and Eve after their sin because he wanted to find them. Sin plunges us under a covering of shame and guilt which prevents us walking openly with God. It is shame that makes us feel hidden from God. God reveals sin, not to condemn us but to bring us into freedom. In one of his podcasts Wayne Jacobsen says that Father God is the safest person we can go to when we've sinned! If we confess our sin he will forgive us and cleanse us from all unrighteousness (1 John 1:8-9). If we can take the step of bringing things into the open with close friends and with him then we can be cleansed of our sin (1 John 1:7).

If we think of repentance only as being a ticket to Heaven and a way of avoiding Hell we miss the point. Repentance is the way into relationship. When we are born again we become children of God (John 1:12). Many of us hold on to the 'escape Hell ticket' rather than entering into the freedom of relationship which we are promised and that we shall look at in chapter 11.

It is tempting to spend a lifetime trying to sort out all the hindrances. That is soul destroying! Remember God's desire to Father you is greater than your desire to seek him. He pursues us but never forces his will on to us. The best way to deal with the hindrances is to pursue him out of desire not duty and seek relationship rather than religion.

Chapter 6

Forgiveness From The Heart

At the end of World War II orphan babies from Europe were sent to North America for medical care. Some of them were placed in a hospital in New York which had all the latest medical equipment and a very sterile environment. The others were sent to Mexico where the hospital equipment was outdated and the surroundings were not very clean.

After a few months both hospitals were checked to see how the babies were progressing. To everyone's surprise the death rate in the New York hospital was much higher than in the Mexican one. Despite the tremendous medical and technological advantage in New York the babies appeared to be better cared for by the Mexican staff. The surveyors investigated further and discovered that in New York the babies were only touched and picked up when they needed something specific e.g. feeding or changing. In Mexico the medical staff were constantly picking the babies up, singing to them, playing with them and expressing tangible forms of affection.

It was abundantly clear that love had made the difference.

God never wanted an institution. He did not form a club and invite people to become members. He has always wanted a family. Being a Father is not something he does, it is who he is.

Adam and Eve were created in love and, before the Fall, experienced perfect love. This was God's intention for us all. We were meant to live all our days experiencing perfect, unconditional love. We were not meant to experience pain or rejection; the perfect love we received we were meant to pass on to the next generation.

As we know, everything went wrong as a result of the Fall and suddenly we were unable to give or receive love in the way God had intended. In fact, our innate expectation and need of love could no longer be satisfied. God's plan had been that our parents would model the love that he has for us. He had intended our mothers to nurture and care for us, and to impart warmth and tenderness in a full and complete way. He had intended our fathers to give us an identity and affirm our place in the world.

All of this was tainted by the Fall. Mothers and fathers struggling with their own pain inevitably passed it on to their children. The perfection God had created was destroyed and what had been complete became tarnished. And so, instead of having a perfect understanding of God and being able to receive his Father's love, we respond to the wounds we receive by building walls in our hearts which prevent us entering the full experience of his love. We try to protect ourselves from further pain by closing our hearts. And so our responses to our damaged relationships with our parents impair our relationship with God. It is important to understand that the issue is not so much the way our parents treat us, as our response to that treatment.

The good news is that the Father wants to restore relationships between parents and children. He also wants us to come to him as the perfect Father.

Martin Luther said: "I have difficulty praying the Lord's prayer because whenever I say 'Our Father', I think of my father who was hard, unyielding and relentless. I cannot help but think of God in that way."[1]

This is where forgiveness comes in. Hanging on to the pain and hurt we have received leads to bitterness. There is a way to offload the pain we have suffered and that is the way of forgiveness.

When Jesus spoke about forgiveness he spoke about forgiving from the heart. Let's look at a familiar story he told:

The Parable of the Unmerciful Servant
Then Peter came to Jesus and asked, "Lord, how many times shall I forgive my brother when he sins against me? Up to seven times?" Jesus answered, "I tell you, not seven times, but seventy-seven times. Therefore, the kingdom of heaven is like a king who wanted to settle accounts with his servants. As he began the settlement, a man who owed him ten thousand talents was brought to him. Since he

was not able to pay, the master ordered that he and his wife and his children and all that he had be sold to repay the debt. The servant fell on his knees before him. 'Be patient with me,' he begged, 'and I will pay back everything.' The servant's master took pity on him, cancelled the debt and let him go. But when that servant went out, he found one of his fellow-servants who owed him a hundred denarii. He grabbed him and began to choke him. 'Pay back what you owe me!' he demanded. His fellow- servant fell to his knees and begged him, 'Be patient with me, and I will pay you back.' But he refused. Instead, he went off and had the man thrown into prison until he could pay the debt. When the other servants saw what had happened, they were greatly distressed and went and told their master everything that had happened. Then the master called the servant in. 'You wicked servant,' he said, 'I cancelled all that debt of yours because you begged me to. Shouldn't you have had mercy on your fellow-servant just as I had on you?' In anger his master turned him over to the jailers to be tortured, until he should pay back all he owed. This is how my heavenly Father will treat each of you unless you forgive your brother from your heart." (Matthew 18:21-35 NIV)

As we consider this story I would like you to think of yourself as the king. We normally look at ourselves as the servant who has been forgiven much. That, of course, is true. We have had our sins utterly and totally forgiven. We, who did not deserve forgiveness, have received it as a free gift from our loving Father. But for the purpose of this chapter I would like you to be the king. It is the king, after all, who is doing the forgiving in the story because he was the one who wanted to settle the outstanding accounts.

Jesus tells the story in response to a question from Peter, "How many times shall I forgive my brother?" Peter comes up with the generous answer of seven! Jesus corrects him with the exaggerated reply of "not seven, but seventy seven times". Jesus is not giving Peter an exact answer. He is making the point that it is not the number that matters but the attitude in which forgiveness is made.

The king had lent a servant some money and now he wanted it repaid. The servant was called to give account of the debt and make repayment. Sadly, the amount was too large and the servant was not in a position to repay his master. In order to reclaim the amount owed to him the king ordered that the servant and all his family be sold. The servant begged for mercy and the king forgave him. In the parable the debt was so large it could never have been repaid. It was more than the servant would earn in his lifetime. Jesus equates the need for forgiveness with having an outstanding debt.

The king had effectively been robbed in that something was taken from him that could never be repaid. He was faced with the choice of seeking (and probably never getting) revenge or letting the servant off. He chose the latter and the servant and his family walked away knowing that the debt was written off, never to be re-claimed.

When we have been wronged or mistreated something has been taken from us that is impossible to get back. We have been violated and it becomes impossible to be repaid. Perhaps parents, school teachers, friends or employers have caused us great pain. They may not know they have done such damage but something has been stolen from us which we can never get back.

Before the king could forgive the servant he had to count the cost of what he had lost. He had to know exactly what had been taken from him. We, too, have to know what has been taken from us. We have to count the cost. Forgiveness does not come cheap. There is a price and we have to know what that price is. Like the king, we have to draw up an inventory of the things that have been taken from us. It is like looking in our wallet and realising that a friend has taken £20. If our friend comes to us and admits taking it we can forgive him. What, though, if our friend also took a credit card and ran up a huge debt on that. We cannot forgive him until we get the credit card statement and see exactly what has been taken. We can only forgive what we know.

So, we need to know what we have lost. What have our parents, teachers, friends or employers taken from us? What have we lost that we can never get back? Only when we have taken stock of those things can we start the process of forgiveness. Like the king, we need to settle our accounts. We need to look at what has been stolen and realise that it is impossible for it to be repaid. Then we need to let it go.

Forgiveness is releasing the debt and letting it go, knowing that we will never get it back. Sometimes it can be painful to count the cost and start the process of letting go. But if we don't it will have a hold over us, continuing to torment and poison our lives. If we release the issue and pain to God then we can be free from its hold over us. We can have a new attitude towards the person who has wronged us because they no longer have a hold over us.

What about the rest of the story? The servant who has been forgiven goes out and tries to seek justice from a fellow servant by demanding the small amount owed to him. He who had received mercy was unable to show mercy to another. This reminds us of the need for us to forgive others just as we have been forgiven (Matthew 6:12, 14-15).

Jesus talked about forgiveness from the heart. He is not concerned with how often we say the words but about the attitude of our hearts. This is why Peter receives an exaggerated reply to his question. If forgiveness is from the heart then it may only need to be said once. If it is not from the heart it does not matter how many times it is said. Your heart will only be free when the cost has been counted and you have resolved to let the matter go.

In a survey, parents were asked what they thought their children would need to forgive them for. Then the children were asked what they actually needed to forgive their parents for. Surprisingly, the things the parents named were not the uppermost issues for their children. When the survey was done the other way round the results were the same. The children wanted to be forgiven for things which had not crossed the parents' minds. This shows how personal the issue is and how much it is a matter of the individual's heart.

When we forgive from our hearts we are choosing to let go of the pain we have received. We release the person (or people) who wronged us and we are able to move on. Although we have been wounded by the actions, words or attitudes of others, they may be totally unaware of the pain they have caused. It is therefore unwise, in most cases, to go to that person and announce that they are forgiven. The fact that they need to be forgiven may come as a complete surprise and may cause them pain. The forgiveness which Jesus is talking about is from the heart and as we release forgiveness, the parts of our hearts which have been closed begin to open up and allow us to receive the Father's love in a greater way.

If we need to go to others and ask for their forgiveness we should do so with a humble and gentle attitude. We need to be specific in order that they know exactly what they are forgiving us for. A blanket request which covers everything we may have ever done wrong does not allow them to forgive us from their heart. As we are specific, they can count the cost and allow the debt to be settled once and for all. As Jesus reminds us in the parable forgiveness is a two way thing.

Jesus said that if we are unwilling to forgive we cannot be forgiven. I believe he is saying that if we do not forgive from the heart then that part of our heart will remain closed and we will be unable to know the full effect of the forgiveness we have received. Of course our sins are forgiven but we may be unable to receive, in our heart, the full impact of that forgiveness.

When we give this teaching at our week long Father-heart encounters we pause at this point and give people time to let these issues come to the surface. We ask them to consider prayerfully who they need to forgive and to count the cost of the things that have been stolen from them. Then we encourage them to ask God to give them the grace to forgive from the heart. This can be a painful and emotional experience but also the start of a process which leads to freedom from things that have held them captive for many years.

I believe in the power of God to work instant miracles. I believe we have a Father who can set us free instantly from the pain and heartache we have carried. But I also believe in process. As you forgive from your heart, expect God to do something for you. Expect to feel a freedom in your spirit but also be aware that you have taken another (big) step on your lifelong journey of living in love - another step towards allowing your heart to be healed and filled with his love.

Notes:
1. Robert Wresch: Church History 3 on Martin Luther

Chapter 7

The Heart of Sonship

"Yet to all who received him, he gave the right to become children of God"
(John 1:12)

A couple of years ago I woke suddenly in the middle of the night with "S.O.S" going round in my mind. Immediately I thought that someone in my family was in danger and I needed to pray for him or her. I went through all my children (whom I knew were safely tucked up in bed), then through my wider family and then through all my friends and work colleagues. As I prayed for them I did not feel any sense of peace that I had found the right person. After a while (and being a bit slow in the middle of the night) I sensed the Father might want to say something to me. Instead of lying awake trying to find the person in need I said what Samuel had done centuries before. "Father, speak for I am listening".

He said three simple words to me: "Slaves, Orphans and Sons". To which my response was a questioning and tentative, "Er Yes?...".

God started to speak to me about his desire for sons. All too often the thrust of Christian mission has been to see people saved, receive a ticket to heaven and be able to escape hell. Forgiveness and the promise of heaven are wonderful gifts of grace, but they are not the whole story. This limited understanding of salvation leaves people as spiritual orphans. It does not help them find their true destiny as God's sons and daughters who have been delivered from the power of darkness and transferred to the kingdom of his beloved Son.

Before we explore the heart of a son, let's look at the nature of a slave and an orphan.

A slave belongs to someone else and as such has no rights or freedom of his own. He is totally controlled by the desires of another. He has to do what he is told when it suits his master rather than at the time of his own choosing. He cannot take a holiday when he wants to; in fact he would be lucky to have any time off at all! Time off is a luxury rather than a right. All initiative is stolen from a slave and he becomes an object in his master's hand, a person without a personality!

The book of Galatians tells us that Christians were once slaves to the law but have been set free through the redeeming work of Jesus. We have been taken from slavery and brought into sonship. As Paul says in Romans 8, it is a glorious sonship. No matter how hard we try, we cannot break away from this old life by our own efforts. The work of Jesus on the cross sets us free from the empty, going-nowhere life of a slave and gives us full life in him.

Under the law a slave had no right to build up an inheritance for himself or his family. All he could be sure of was his board and lodgings, and even that was at risk if he could not work because of injury, sickness or old age. All he could do was live by the rules and this was like dancing on hot coals with no chance to settle and feel at rest. When you take out a financial investment, you are often told (in the small print) that past performance is no guarantee to future success. So it is for a slave. All his past performance and his hard work will not guarantee him any rest or comfort for the future. It is work, work, work!

The life of a slave is a miserable one. And so is the life of an orphan.

An orphan has no identity, no name, no family and no inheritance. Whereas a slave is bound to another, an orphan can try to make something happen for himself. Because nothing has been done for him, the orphan has to fight for everything he needs or wants. He has to make a name for himself and strive to gain position, possessions and pride. Once he has them, he is not going to let them go. At all costs he will hold on to them for they are his! An orphan cannot give freely because he has no guarantee that what he gives will be replaced. He is like the worker in the parable who buried his talent in the ground rather than investing it in the bank. He can trust no-one to look after it on his behalf, so he holds on to it rather than releasing it to grow and prosper.

An orphan believes his value and approval are based on what he has done or achieved rather than on who he is. He cannot enjoy friendship or relationship as he is competing with everyone else to gain their approval through his own actions or attainments. It is very tiring being an orphan, having to rely entirely on your own energy and effort.

In the church today there are many spiritual orphans. There are those who have been led out of slavery but have never been introduced to a loving Father. This is where my "SOS" comes in. I felt God say to me during that night that there were many people who are born again but then left as orphans. They cross one threshold but are never taken across the next into sonship and so they live out their Christian lives under a cloud of performance, duty and restless activity. Rather than enjoying a relationship with the Father, as Jesus did, they strive for position, rank or function. They start to climb the ladder of success in the church and often push others off to advance their own journey. They are takers not givers and, when they become leaders, they lead with control and manipulation rather than love and nurture.

When Adam and Eve were driven from the garden, they walked out of the nurture and love of the Father and started a journey where they had to work for everything they needed. They left the safety of the Father's provision and care and had to provide for themselves. Suddenly they had to rely on to their own resources and initiative. It all depended on them (or so they thought). In Genesis 4, after killing Abel, Cain became a "restless wanderer", a man with no place to rest or stay, making his own way through life. He truly had the heart of an orphan.

After the Fall the heart of man entered an orphan state and this is the case for each of us today.

There is a desire in all of us to try and make it on our own. We attempt to build our own empires and kingdoms which we hope will stand the test of time. In the world we see people work long hours for a demanding boss, but the goal posts move frequently and they have to try harder to please and to achieve. Sadly, we see this in the church as well. Instead of being a haven and a resting place, church often encourages the same striving and performance as is endemic in the world. People are beaten up enough at work. They don't want to give up their free time to be beaten up even more.

But we can take heart. This is not the whole story. The final "S" in SOS is for sonship and highlights the desire in the Father's heart to bring us all home.

God promises to be a Father to the fatherless (Psalm 68:5) and that he will not leave us as orphans (John 14:18).

Let's not leave people as orphans. Let's help bring them into the glorious freedom of the sons of God. But to do so, we ourselves need to have the heart of a son and where better to look than at the life of Jesus.

There is an amazing passage in Luke 2 when the twelve year old Jesus stays in the temple at the end of the Passover feast to talk to the teachers and leaders. When Joseph and Mary eventually find him he says: *"How is it that you had to look for me? Did you not see and know that it is necessary for me to be in my Father's house and about my Father's business?"* (Luke 2:49-51

AMP). To Jesus, it was the most natural thing to be in his Father's house doing what his Father was doing. Mary and Joseph could not understand this, and despite his desire to start his Heavenly Father's business, Jesus submitted to his earthly parents, returned to Nazareth and went back to work in the carpenter's shop. He served them faithfully for another eighteen years until he started what we call his ministry.

Jesus' example of submission shows he was prepared to lay aside his own will and desire. He had spent eternity being a son to the Father; he knew what it meant to have the heart of a son and to do his Father's will. It was, therefore, natural for him to have the same heart towards Joseph and Mary.

As well as being a son to Joseph and Mary, Jesus was also known as the son of David. This speaks to us of spiritual sonship. He was following in the footsteps of the great king who was known as a man after God's heart, a man who loved to worship and who was gentle and intimate. David had his weaknesses and we know about his failures, but he was the man that God said would have children sitting on his throne forever. What David showed, Jesus revealed more fully. Jesus, too was a man in intimate relationship with the Father. He was a worshipper. He was gentle and loving. And now he sits on that throne as the King of kings.

Jesus was also known as the son of God. In fact it was his sonship (rather than his miracles or deeds) that defined his life. At his baptism, before he had started his public ministry, the

Father spoke from Heaven and affirmed his love for Jesus simply as his son. Sonship was the key issue that the Devil tried to undermine when he tempted Jesus in the wilderness. As ever, the Deceiver tried to use the truth to manipulate his own ends. "If you are the son of God....." (Matthew 4:3,6) were the words he used. Jesus was the son of God and he could have done any of the things the Devil asked of him but he refused to submit his spirit to the manipulation and control of Satan. On the mountain when Jesus was transfigured the Father spoke once again from Heaven and re-affirmed Jesus as the son he loves.

It was sonship that became a stumbling block to the Pharisees and the teachers of the law. Jesus' claim to be the son of God made them really angry and caused them, on several occasions, to try and kill him.

Jesus' sole desire was to please his Father. Everything he did or said was because his Father had told him what to do and say. He was in such close communication with the Father that it was natural for him to do what the Father did, go where the Father went and say what the Father said. In the Psalms it is said prophetically of Jesus that it was his delight to do the Father's will (Psalm 40:8). Jesus said of himself that he could do nothing on his own for he was so dependent on his Father and desirous of doing his will that the life of the Father flowed through him.

Sonship defined Jesus' life. It defined who he was and through it he shows us the heart of a son, pleasing the Father and living for him. To Jesus this was not subservience but total freedom. It was the full life that he describes in John 10:10.

Jesus shows us the tremendous difference between being a son *of* someone and being a son *to* someone. We are all somebody's son or daughter. You may not know or live with your natural father but nonetheless you are his child (whether you like it or not). Being someone's son or daughter is a natural fact we cannot get away from. Being a son to someone is an entirely different matter, as this is something that we have the power to change. It is a choice we make and once made it can influence our lives in very significant ways.

The heart of sonship opens the door to three wonderful things which a slave or orphan never receives - inheritance, freedom and identity.

As sons we receive an inheritance from Father. All that is his becomes ours. We no longer need to strive for possessions or position. We no longer have to 'work our socks off' for something to hold on to. An inheritance is given freely to us through Jesus and all that was his (by right) he gives to us through grace. In Luke 15 the father in the story tells the elder son that everything belonging to him also belongs to his son, yet the elder son was unable to accept and enjoy it. An inheritance is a valuable thing. It is far more than the sum of the goods or monetary value passed from one generation to the next. It represents someone's life and work, his or her very soul. It is not something to be taken lightly or squandered. An inheritance truly is a treasure.

As sons we are entitled to freedom and this is something a slave or orphan can never enjoy. When Jesus was in the temple announcing his ministry, he declared that he had come to set the captives free. He sets us free from the yoke of slavery (whether it's addiction, lust, performance, people-pleasing, fear, pride, or religious duty) and leads us into a wonderful easy yoke of relationship. Jesus waves a banner for freedom and declares that the children of God shall be free! In John 8 he contrasts the position of a slave and a son:

> *"So if the Son sets you free, you will be free indeed!"* (verse 36)

A son is truly free. He is no longer held in bondage to sin or the demands of the law. He is free, completely free - free to make decisions, free to enjoy a relationship based on mutual love and trust, rather than based on orders and control. Jesus says that a son will have a place in the family forever. A slave could only dream of this but a son has a rightful place in the family and is involved in decision making along with and on behalf of the Father. This is the life of freedom Jesus offers. In Galatians 5 Paul says *"it was for freedom that we were set free"*. This might sound a funny thing to say on first reading but the truth is that we were set free for no other reason but than to enjoy the same freedom as Jesus enjoyed.

Our freedom is described as a "glorious freedom" (Romans 8:21). It is a glorious freedom that the whole world is groaning or straining to catch hold of. Creation is suffering from bondage to decay and destruction and is longing for the day when it will find the same freedom as that enjoyed by the sons of God. The destruction of the planet, the floods, the famine and the inequality all around us, contrast with the real freedom promised to us by our Father. As we become free, so the world around us will find freedom. As we are free so, I believe, the natural world will find freedom and some of the destruction we see around us will be reversed.

Sons have an identity. Have you ever read some of the genealogies in the Bible? What were they put there for? What you see as you read them is that everybody was someone's son!

Sonship defined Jesus and his ministry. He healed the sick, preached and prophesied but all these things were done out of his relationship and closeness to the Father. He did nothing without hearing from his Father first. The most important thing to Jesus was not his function or duty but this relationship. He was a true son. That relationship is ours to enjoy as well. We are sons and daughters of the Father and can enjoy the same relationship with God that Jesus enjoyed. This is not an add-on or optional extra. It was what we were made for. *"Because you are sons, God sent the Spirit of his Son into our hearts, the Spirit who calls out 'Abba, Father'. So you are no longer a slave but a son."* (Galatians 4:6-7)

Having the heart of a son means we are attracted to the Father. Think of a magnet. Depending which way it is placed it will either attract or repel. An orphan repels as he seeks to push himself away from the Father's love. Whenever the Father draws close he bounces off in the other direction. Turn the magnet round and it instantly attaches itself to the other object. A son is like that. He is attracted by the Father's love. Psalm 40:6-8 catch hold of the heart of a son; *"I desire to do your will, O my God, your law is written in my heart"*. As sonship becomes part of us so we desire to do the Father's will. Obedience is no longer a struggle or something that we have to do. It becomes natural because we do it from our heart and out of love.

The Father longs to welcome you back to him and back to your real home. We are no longer orphans but sons. We can choose to stay with relief from slavery and sin or to enter into the fullness of relationship that is ours through grace. SOS really can be a matter of life or death. You were born to be a son or daughter. Don't settle for less.

In the next chapter we will explore this more fully through a familiar story.

Chapter 8

A Father and His Sons

"There was a man who had two sons.
The younger one said to his father,
'father give me my share of the
estate'. So he divided his property
between them."
(Luke 15:11-12)

The story of the lost son, or the prodigal son, as we have come to know it, is one of the best known in the Bible. It is a story about the Father's heart and his extravagant love. It tells of God's overwhelming desire for relationship with his children despite their failings and shortcomings and it is also a story about **our** hearts.

In the last chapter we saw how the Father longs for sons and daughters who live in intimate relationship with him and who delight to be in his presence. Father's desire is that we would throw off the shackles of religion and obligation and live a grace-filled life of relationship with him.

Let's look at the two sons in the story and see how this may work out.

The Younger Son
He wanted his inheritance! He wanted it so much that he was prepared to dishonour his father and dare to ask for it before his father had even died.

A Father And His Sons

I imagine that he did not wake up one morning and decide on impulse to ask his father for a share of the estate. I guess he had plotted and schemed for months. Frustrated in his work on the farm, looking at the money in the bank and dreaming of all the things he could do, he finally decided to take what would be his and embark on a life of freedom.

All he really wanted was to satisfy his own desires. There was no thought of honour for his father or loyalty to his brother. He wanted to please himself, go wherever he wished, live the sort of life he chose and control his own destiny. It was a very selfish decision.

He must have known it was not his right to ask for his share and he valued that right more than the relationship with his father or with the rest of his family. Of course we know it was not his right, but in the blindness of his heart he did not see that because all he wanted was to please himself. I often ask myself, as a father, what I would have done. I don't think I would have given in and let him have what he asked for. I might have sat down with him and tried to talk to him or maybe given him a monthly allowance and helped him budget. However, the father divided the estate between both his sons and let the younger one go off on his own way. The story gives us no clue whether he tried to dissuade him or talk him out of it. Then a short time later the son took himself off to a distant land where he spent everything. In his heart he had stopped being his father's son and taken control of his own life in order that he could live it his way.

We don't know how long it was before the son ran out of money. All we know is that while he had money he had 'friends' – people who hung on to him for what they could get. They gathered round him like vultures around a carcass. All they wanted was for him to buy the next round of drinks, throw the next party or allow them to indulge in even more depravity. When the money ran out they were nowhere to be seen. Like vultures they left the skeleton on the ground and moved on to the next naive victim.

Finally, the son decided to go home and seek employment in his father's house, not as a son but as a servant. His 'gimme' attitude had become a 'change me' attitude. He was in a place where he could begin to change and start to seek forgiveness. He could not yet believe he would be restored to the family. All he sought was a job, some food and shelter and maybe the start of reconciliation and acceptance by his father. How surprised he must have been when his father ran out to meet him. Perhaps he thought he was about to receive all the punishment he deserved!

The Elder Son
One thing we often forget is that the elder son also received his inheritance. The story tells us that the father divided his estate between both his sons.

As the younger son went off in rebellion the elder one stayed at home and worked on the farm. When his brother returned he was very angry. The apparent injustice pours out: "I've *always* worked for you; you've never given me anything", he complains to his father. In his concern for fairness and justice he forgets that he, too, had received his share of the inheritance. In his heart he had never been able to receive what his father had given him. He was locked into a cycle of work, performance and duty. His father had been generous with both his sons and although the elder son did not go off and waste his share, neither did he receive or value what had been given to him.

Just as the father went out to meet the younger son, so he went out to the elder one and tried to talk to him. He wanted to draw him into the centre of his heart. As far as we know the elder son didn't yield or come in to join the celebration.

The elder son had also stopped being a son to his father. In his heart he did not value their relationship. He, too, was looking out for his own interests but he expressed it in a dutiful religious way, whereas his younger brother expressed it in rebellion and sin.

Both sons had such a limited understanding of their father's generosity and love towards them. Both felt they had to *earn* it.

The Father
The father could have withheld the inheritance from the younger son. He could have made him stay at home and continue working on the farm. If he had held him back, what would that have done to his heart? I guess it might have made him harder, more set in rebellion and against his father. The father made the hardest decision of his life – to let his son go but he watched and waited for the day that he would he return.

When that day came he did not march his son inside and insist on him having a bath before welcoming him back. No, he threw his arms around the filthy, sweaty man and covered his dirt with a robe. He gave him a ring to signify the family's authority and shoes for his feet. Whilst the son had stopped being a son, the father had never stopped being a father. His unconditional love welcomed his son back into the family despite his filth and shame.

The father's heart was also completely open to his elder son. He went out to draw him into the family and the celebration, to remind him that he, too, had received an inheritance. 'My son,' he said, 'you are always with me, and everything I have is yours' (verse 31).

Both sons lived like slaves. One was a slave to self-indulgence and the other to duty and obligation.

Jesus uses this story to expose our hearts and give us the opportunity to consider where we stand with the Father. Are we entrenched in sin? Are we living a life of religious duty? Neither will satisfy and Jesus offers us another way.

For all of us there is a way back to relationship with the Father, a relationship which is not based on duty, performance or obligation, nor dependent on us living a sin-free life. It is a relationship where we are accepted for who we are, not for what we have done. Many people in churches today feel they cannot draw close to God because of the shame of past (or present) sin. They feel distant or hopeless and believe they have no chance of drawing near to the Father's heart. Others think that if they can only live a life filled with duty and service then they may have a chance of winning the Father's favour. Either way we can become trapped in desperation and feel distant from the Father.

The story of the two sons and their extravagantly loving Father gives us hope. Jesus shows us that there is a Father waiting for us. He longs for his sons and daughters to find their way home so that their sin and shame can be covered and they can receive the kiss of the Father's favour.

None of us have to remain outside Father's wonderful love. We can all experience it. We can all come home.

In John 14:1-3 we are told of a place prepared for each one of us in the Father's presence. This is not only a picture of our eternal home, but a statement of God's intention to dwell with us NOW. In verse 23 of the same chapter Jesus reinforces this for us: "If anyone loves me, he will obey my teaching, my Father will love him and we will come to him and *make our home with him*" (emphasis added). The Father seeks us out to welcome us home and then make his home in our hearts. This is not something we earn through our service or performance but is a free gift won for us by Jesus. It is our inheritance. Jesus showed us how to be a perfect son. He only did his Father's will as he lived each day in his presence.

All of us can experience this homecoming. We can all receive the Father's unconditional love which is showered on us freely and not earned through good works or tiring efforts. Can we lay down the striving and struggle of our Christian lives and find rest in him? As we receive his love our relationship with the Father will be renewed.

This story asks a question of us all. Are we slaves or sons? A slave can only introduce others to a master whereas a son reveals a Father.

Whether we are struggling with sin, or sinking under duty and performance, there is a Father who is watching and waiting. He is longing for the day when sons and daughters will return and find their home with him. He is longing for the opportunity to throw a robe around our shoulders and embrace us. He is the Father who is always coming out to meet us. He longs to say "Welcome home".

Chapter 9

A Childlike Heart

Jesus is full of surprises! He taught with gentleness and compassion. He spoke about a new kingdom of love rather than one of aggression and force. He spent time with the marginalised and the poor rather than with leaders or those with power and influence.

At the end of one of his teachings he gives us a vital clue about how we can enter this new kingdom. We have to change, humble ourselves and become as little children (Matthew 18:3-4). This must have shocked Jesus' listeners! How liberating! No longer are there endless requirements of "do's" and "don'ts"; no longer are there impossible regulations to be fulfilled. All we need to do is to come like little children.

Although a liberating statement, it was one many of Jesus' listeners found too hard. They were unable to lay aside their own strength and abilities to find this mysterious way of entering the kingdom. The simplicity of the gospel can sometimes seem too hard or carry too great a cost, as it was for the rich young man (Matthew 19:16-22). When he asked what he had to **do** to earn eternal life, Jesus invited him to give up both the wealth and religious observance on which he relied. He was invited to learn from Jesus how to live in childlike dependence on a loving heavenly Father who gives his children the 'treasures of heaven' (Matthew 6:20 and Colossians 2:3).

We wonder why we are worn out and tired when Jesus promises us a life of rest! Often it is because we are trying to do things in our strength rather than following his guidance (and example) of becoming like a child.

Let's look at some characteristics of children and then see how this can apply to us.

Children are Trusting

Children simply believe that their parents will provide all their needs! They don't worry where the next meal will come from or how clean clothes find their way back into the cupboard. They trust that when something is needed it will be given. They have little or no concept of the work that goes into the cooking or cleaning or even the entertainment which is provided by TV, DVDs or the books that contain that 'bed-time story'.

To children everything seems to turn up on demand. Their parents often seem to be able to discern their needs and provide everything at exactly the right time.

Young children particularly have a simple, yet profound, level of trust. We lose this quality as we grow older and become more aware of the need to question and be suspicious of others' motives.

Psalm 22:9 reminds us that God made us with this simple childlike trust. As a child trusts in his parents, so God wants us to trust in him for all our needs. He, as the perfect Father, can supply everything we need, when we need it. He is completely consistent and completely trustworthy.

Children are Dependent

Children's lives are in someone else's hands. They depend on others to be there for them and to be consistent and safe. They rely on parents to collect them from school and then to feed them. They need to be provided for and loved. When parents aren't dependable a child has nowhere else to turn.

As we grow up we learn to depend more on our own strength and abilities. There is a right independence which is part of growing up. We learn to dress ourselves, to cross roads safely, and take more responsibility for the decisions we make. However, there is another independence which arises from the rebellion caused by our fallen state. Within us there is an attitude of "I want to do things my way" or "I can't trust others". It is this independence Jesus addresses when he asks us to become like children.

God calls us to depend on him (Matthew 6:25-33) for he is totally dependable. He will never let us down as he is always there for us. There is nowhere we can go that takes us outside his love or presence. There is no situation that we cannot give over to him. He is totally reliable.

Children are Carefree
Children do not carry out a risk assessment before each new activity! They have a go without thinking of the consequences. They only worry about falling flat on their faces when it happens. Fear of the unknown can paralyse us and prevent us from taking those carefree steps of faith.

Because our Father is so dependable we can be carefree in his presence. The resources of Heaven are at our disposal, so we can take risks of faith. God is not interested in a polished performance where everything is planned and thought out in advance. He wants his children to be free in his presence. He wants us to have the freedom that comes from knowing and experiencing his loving care for us.

We can, quite simply, cast our cares on to him because he cares for us and has promised not to let us fall (1 Peter 5:7, Psalm 55:2).

Children are Innocent
Innocence is unspoilt simplicity. Children do not hide themselves behind a façade of protective layers. They wear their hearts on their sleeves! As adults we spend too much time seeking popularity or pleasing others by hiding our real selves away. Children don't have those pretences. They think nothing of bursting into a room and running to their parents to show or tell the latest triumph. They are unconcerned about the response or the reproach which may follow. They simply see things as they are.

In our Father's presence we can remove the veils. His love will bring us into a level of security that enables us to regain the unspoilt simplicity we so easily lose.

Children Need to be Loved

We were made to be loved. We are all born with a need for constant love and affection. Because our parents can't give us all the love we needed as children, we enter adult life with a "love deficit" which causes us to look for love elsewhere. There are many false lovers in the world today and without the proper foundation of love we will chase after them in order to satisfy our need for love.

God is love. When we come to him we come to love. 1 John 3:1 says God *lavishes* his love on us. As a child needs love so we all need to know and receive the perfect love of our Father.

Children Need Their Parents

Children need direction and discipline from their parents as much as they need their love, nurture and care. Parents guide children through a challenging world, providing boundaries where necessary, and releasing them when and where appropriate.

As the Father's children we need his direction and discipline as well as his love, nurture and care. We need the boundaries he sets and the freedom which he gives us. When we try to make it on our own we set ourselves up for disappointment and burn-out.

Children Imitate Their Parents

Have you ever turned round and seen one of your children imitating you? How often we see them copy our mannerisms and use our favourite phrases, especially, or so it seems, the most annoying ones! That's what children do; they are always watching and they learn far more from what we do than what we say.

This is what Jesus did! He did what he saw his Father doing and he said what he heard his Father saying. It really was 'like Father, like son'! Paul exhorts us to be imitators of God and live a life of love (Ephesians 5:1).

Children Use Their Imagination

They dream BIG dreams! In a child's creative mind nothing is impossible. They can go to the moon and back in a wheelbarrow. The hero can go endless miles through many battles and much hardship to rescue his princess. Children are full of creativity and imagination but sadly this is often dulled over the years.

But our Father is able to do far more than we can ask or even imagine (Ephesians 3:20-21). He has a BIG plan for us (1 Corinthians 2:9-10). He wants to revitalise our imagination and creativity.

Children Know How to Rest

They race around madly all day and are constantly on the go, wearing their parents out. But at night, as soon as their heads touch the pillow, they fall asleep! When activity becomes too much, children know to run inside and climb on to a father or mother's lap. They know how to find rest, an ability we, as adults, so easily lose.

Jesus lived a busy and full life. He faced the same pressures we face but he took time to be with his Father. He removed himself from the pressure and rested. This was not just external or physical rest. His heart was at rest because he knew who his Father was! He was so at rest that he could sleep through a storm at sea in a small open boat.

Rest so often eludes us but it is what Jesus promised. The Message puts it well:

> *"Are you tired? Worn out? Burned out on religion? Come to me. Get away with me and you'll recover your life. I'll show you how to take a real rest. Walk with me and work with me - watch how I do it. Learn the unforced rhythms of grace. I won't lay anything heavy or ill-fitting on you. Keep company with me and you'll learn to live freely and lightly." (Matthew 11:28-30)*

Children Are Never Satisfied

They always want more and have no fear in coming back to ask for it!

Jesus makes us an offer. If we are thirsty we can come and drink. If we ask for a drink then streams of living water will flow from us. The same invitation is given through the prophet Isaiah; *"Come, all you who are thirsty, come to the water; and you who have no money, come, buy and eat! Come, buy wine and milk without money and without cost"* (chapter 55:1-2). Don't settle for the things that won't satisfy; pursue and desire the life that comes from God. It is an unending stream of life.

*****

Jesus said we had to *change*, humble ourselves and become like children. For us to enter the inheritance we are promised we have to change and let go of our sophistication, our striving, our plans and our programmes. We have to stop trying to find our identity in 'doing' and instead find it in 'being' a son or daughter to the Father. To step back from all of the things which we do in our own strength and motivation requires a humbling and a letting go of our pride and independence. We can learn to live in love rather than activity. We can learn that out of simplicity comes a power which we have not experienced or seen before. We find that God's power is perfected in our weakness. In Surprised by the Power of the Spirit Jack Deere writes: "The miraculous ministry of Jesus was absolutely dependent on his intimacy with the Father"[1].

This is a simple, yet powerful, way to live. It is the way Jesus lived and we know the extraordinary things that happened through him.

This is hard for many people. It is not easy to let go. It is not easy to be humbled before peers or family. Embracing a childlike heart may not be our default setting but it is the key to living as Jesus lived. The kingdom of God is the inheritance for the Father's sons and daughters. It is not given to slaves but to sons. It is not given to the strong but to the weak.

In the next chapter we will explore weakness in more detail.

Notes:
1. Surprised by the Power of the Spirit - page 152, Jack Deere

Chapter 10

Carried By Our Father

"The LORD your God, who is going before you, will fight for you, as he did for you in Egypt, before your very eyes, and in the desert. There you saw how the LORD your God carried you, as a father carries his son, all the way you went until you reached this place." (Deuteronomy 1:30-31 NIV)

We live in a competitive society. Schools, colleges, sport, and even families push us to be the best. We have to fight to be the top of the pile. We are taught that any indication of weakness is wrong. Sadly, this driven lifestyle spills over into our Christian lives. We think of all the things **we** can do for God - as if he needs our helping hand! We may think that we can earn his favour with our activity and that our religious duty will lead to his blessing or will catch his attention.

The biblical reality is very different. Our relationship with God is not dependent on our efforts but totally dependent on him.

The verses quoted at the start of this chapter give us a beautiful insight into the Father's heart. Moses is retelling the Israelites their story: how they were set free from captivity in Egypt, crossed the Red Sea and were led through the desert to the promised land. Moses explains to the people the faithfulness of God and his extraordinary provision for them.

The story of the Israelite nation was one of amazing miracles and the incredible intervention of a great God. He defeated Pharaoh, parted the Red Sea and provided food and water in a barren desert. Shortly after the death of Moses he parted the River Jordan and then won a supernatural military battle against the city of Jericho. Here was a God who did everything for his people. All they had to do was place their trust in him.

Moses tells the people not to be afraid because God has gone before them and has fought for them. He has carried them as a father carries a son ALL the way until they reached 'this place'.

At the end of Moses' life we are given another illustration of the Father's desire to carry us. As Moses is blessing the people, just before his death, he reminds them that the everlasting arms of God are always underneath them (Deuteronomy 33:26-27).

What is interesting about these stories is that the people were repeatedly rebelling against God and wanting to go their own way, yet God comes and tenderly says that he will carry them. Similarly, he does not wait for us to sort ourselves out and have our lives in order before he helps us. He is ready and willing to help us in our weakness, independence and rebellion. He carries us because he loves us, not because we have earned it.

We may often think that God wants to lift our burdens and release us from the weight of the things we carry. We might think he will walk alongside us carrying our burdens whilst we run free. God will lift our burdens from us but he will also carry us! In fact he promises to carry us ALL the way. He never grows tired or weary, nor does he need to put us down for a rest. He is entirely capable of carrying us all the way through whatever life may throw at us.

Perhaps we may think that everything is up to us. We think we need to do everything for God in our own strength but his heart is to carry us as he carried the people of Israel. He is a Father who longs to carry his children. As we saw in the previous chapter, we need to change and become as little children in order for this to happen.

Our culture praises strength. But in the end our activity can consume us and leave us exhausted. God knows this which is why he wants to carry us. He knows the limitations of our human nature. He knows the frailty of man and he invites us to fall back into the safety and strength of his arms. Recognising our weakness is the doorway to finding the ultimate source of strength. If we allow ourselves to be carried we will find a place of safety and security.

In Isaiah 40 we have a wonderful picture of the strength and comfort of God. We read about his power and majesty as he measures out oceans and weighs the mountains. We read about the greatness of his mind and the extent of his perception. But we also read of the tender words he speaks to his people and the comfort he shows us. We are given a picture of a great God coming in awesome power (verse 10) but we also see his gentle compassionate heart (verse 11):

> "He tends his flock like a shepherd: he gathers the lambs in his arms and *carries* them close to his heart; he gently leads those that have young" (emphasis added).

He is the all-powerful God yet he carries his chosen ones close to his heart, just as a shepherd carries his lambs.

These are two pictures of the same God and both are completely true. He is Almighty God, the all powerful one who is strong in battle. But if that is the only picture we have of him then in time he will become distant and we will perceive him as angry and judgemental. If we view God only as the one who weighs out mountains and measures the seas we deny ourselves the opportunity of coming close to he who is ultimately the God of love.

This does not mean that God is unconcerned about sin. He hates sin, and that hatred is an expression of his love, because sin destroys the lives of his beloved children and separates them from him. And so he reaches down and embraces us in his arms. As we read in chapter 8 God is a Father who is always willing to welcome his children home and to cover their sin with a robe of righteousness. As we learn to live in love we will hate sin as much as he does.

We have a Father who draws us to himself in love and who cares for us. He nurtures us and showers us with loving kindness. His power is perfected in our weakness. It can be hard to let go of our own strength, since it goes against much of our training and upbringing. But as we do we realise that, in acknowledging our weakness, his strength and power can operate more effectively. As we get out of the way, his glory will shine and people around us will start to see him and his love rather than us and our imperfections.

We may think of Jesus as a strong man who could perform all sorts of amazing miracles. Yet he tells us that he could do nothing on his own because he was totally reliant on his Father. I imagine that as he walked around he was listening to his Father's voice guiding him to the man or woman who needed healing or to the down-trodden who needed to hear his words of life. I wonder if he could have walked on the water without the enabling word of his Father? In Matthew 11 we are given a little insight into Jesus' life. He tells us that the secrets of the Kingdom are not given to the wise and learned – to those who appear to have their act together. They are given to those who, like little children, are weak and open-hearted. Jesus had clearly received these secrets of wisdom and guidance from his Father and so he must have had that childlike heart which he encourages his listeners to seek. Jesus knew what it was to be carried by his Father.

Jesus understood the power of weakness. He knew he could do nothing without hearing from his Father. He knew that, on his own, his 'ministry' would be very limited. He wants us to understand this too, for in John 15:5-8 he says that we can do nothing apart from him. The only way for us to be fruitful is to remain in him as he remains in the Father. A life lived apart from Jesus is like a branch that bears no fruit which is then chopped off and thrown into the fire!

We can learn so much from the life of Jesus. In John 17:24 he prays that we will be where he is. Where is he now? He is at his Father's side, seated at the right hand of God in glory. Hang on! Is Jesus really saying we can be where he is? Can we, too, be at the Father's side? Paul re-enforces this for us in Ephesians. Firstly, he catalogues the wonderful spiritual blessings that are ours through Christ (chapter 1) and then he paints a picture of our new life. We are made alive in Christ and, yes, we are seated with him in the Heavenly realms (Ephesians 2:5).

In fact, it is even more intimate than this. Jesus came from the heart of the Father (John 1:18 NLT). He came from a very safe, warm and comforting place and it is to that same place that he welcomes us. If we live in Christ then we also live in the Father.

It is not the strong or independent who are carried. It is those who know their own weakness who let the Father carry them and who understand that they are loved unconditionally.

Jesus' invitation to come to him (Matthew 11:28) is an invitation to lay aside our own strength and to let go of the desire to make a name for ourselves; to stop building our own kingdoms and simply to come and let him carry us. We may have lost heart always trying to hit the mark and be an acceptable Christian. Deep down we know that we are weak but there is something that drives us to carry on in our own strength. We live with a level of performance that so often breaks us or causes those around to despair because they have no chance of reaching the same level of achievement.

We may wonder why our churches are not growing but if we are not living the life of rest that Jesus promised perhaps we should stop and ask ourselves: 'Would anyone want a life like mine?' John Eldredge describes the modern church as tired, worn out and bored[1]. Why would anyone want to join a 'club' which advocates that sort of lifestyle! Jesus promises us a life of rest: "Come to me, all you who are weary and burdened, and I will give you rest" (Matthew 11:28). This is a free offer but sadly, we don't always choose to accept it.

It is not our words that ultimately affect others but our lifestyle. If we tell people we have chicken pox when we have measles, it will be measles they catch, not chicken pox. Our life is a far more powerful witness than the words we say or the institutions we build.

If we are able to change and are willing to admit our weaknesses, we can let him carry us. What a safe haven we will find. It is then that our lives become the real message of the gospel.

There is a powerful video called Team Hoyt (available on YouTube). Here is a father and son team competing in a triathlon race. The son wanted to enter the race so they trained together for the swimming, running and cycling. A herculean effort for anyone! The day of the race comes and the film opens with the father swimming in the sea with the son behind him in an inflatable dinghy. The father tows the son for over two miles, then cycles for 112 miles on a specially constructed tandem before finally running a marathon pushing the son who sits in his wheelchair. The son is severely disabled. He can't walk or talk yet he has been the inspiration for these superhuman events.

Eventually when they reach the finishing line, the son's face is one huge smile as he waves his arms in a victory salute. He crosses the line and finishes the race. It does not matter to the son that he has done very little except having been towed, carried and pushed by his father. He has the joy and satisfaction of knowing he has completed another triathlon.

This is what Moses is talking about when he says God carries us. All the effort is our Father's but we share the enjoyment of the victory!

Notes:
1. *Waking the Dead - page 7, John Eldredge*

Chapter 11

A Wide Open Space

"So if the Son sets you free, you will be free indeed" (John 8:36 NIV)

I wonder what picture the word 'freedom' conjures up in your mind? For some it may be the film "Braveheart" and the longing in William Wallace's heart for a free Scotland. For others it may be a desire to escape somewhere on your own without any responsibility or worry. Whatever picture we have in our minds freedom is something we all long for.

Freedom is quite difficult to define. Many people will say it is about having the right to do as you please but it is bigger than that. Pope John Paul II said: *"Freedom consists not in doing what we like, but in having the right to do what we ought"*[1]. Freedom is not doing as we please but being totally uninhibited in the life that God has planned for us. Freedom has boundaries which are there to protect rather than restrict us. A train appears to be limited by the railway track but it is the track that provides its very means of freedom. The train can go nowhere without the track. A car would not be able to move freely on a railway track as the rails would inhibit its movement. A car needs a road, a train needs the rails. Freedom does not mean we have to be in control. Instead it means that we are able to hand control over to God, who ultimately is the only one able to fulfil all our desires.

Sadly, our culture has come to praise celebrities whose unlimited wealth allows them to have almost anything they want. Their lifestyle is portrayed in the media as one of complete freedom, as we are led to believe that their money will buy them whatever they wish. They appear to live in a problem-free bubble that the rest of us can only aspire to. Yet there is often despair in their hearts as they realise that money is not the answer to all their needs. We read of broken relationships and an unsettled lifestyle that is clearly not satisfied by apparent unlimited wealth. Interestingly, Mike Tyson said: *"Real freedom is having nothing. I was freer when I didn't have a cent"*[2].

Money certainly is not the key to freedom!

Jesus knew what it was to be free. He was not bound by the restrictions of humanity. Although he had stepped into humanity his life was a richness of extra-human activity in which miracles became the norm. On one of his first public appearances he turned water into a very generous quantity of excellent wine. He fed over 5,000 with just five loaves of bread and two small fish. He walked on water. He could turn a disastrous night's fishing into a bumper catch. He could pay his taxes by finding a coin in a fish's mouth. He healed the lame, the lepers and the blind. He told simple stories that confused the wise and set the listening heart totally free. But true freedom goes beyond the miraculous. It is freedom from bondage to addiction and performance and from the need to be 'right'. It's freedom to forgive and love others whatever the cost. It's freedom from fear, selfish anger and the need to retaliate.

Jesus lived a life of freedom. He was free to be the friend of 'sinners' despite the protests of the religious people. He was free to resist the power of temptation in the desert and in Gethsemane. The freedom he enjoyed is something that he promises us! Freedom is not miraculous activity but the fruit of being secure in our relationship with our Heavenly Father. True freedom is part of our inheritance as the children of God. Jesus tells us that if we know the truth it will set us free (John 8:32) and "if the Son sets you free, you will be free indeed" (John 8:36 NIV). Being set free by Jesus is complete freedom.

Jesus contrasts the life of a slave with that of a son. Slaves never have a place in the family. They are outsiders brought in to serve and do the will of the master. They have no free time of their own as they are always at the beck and call of the one who owns them. A slave has no rights but is totally dependent on the goodwill of the master.

A son is different. He has a place in the family and belongs to it forever. That's why the son in Luke 15 could be welcomed back into the father's house. He was not a slave, nor had he ever been one. He was a rebellious son but when he came home his father welcomed him back into his place in the family.

Slaves are bound; sons are free!

I have said elsewhere in this book that we become sons and daughters when we become Christians. The Bible is very clear that our conversion gives us the full inheritance that Jesus died for. We do not need to go through a second conversion to become sons and daughters. Although we are children of God, many Christians live without that being an experiential reality in their daily lives. I hope, in reading this book, you have started to realise who you really are; that you are no longer trapped as a slave nor an orphan, but that you **are** a son or daughter of your Heavenly Father. This is a revelation that can become a reality in your lives. However, it is not a one-off revelation but an ongoing and growing realisation that God is your Father. It is a transformation from simply knowing 'God is **a** Father' to knowing that 'he is a Father **to me**'. Over time, our understanding of what it means to be a son or daughter can grow and we can leave the milk of infancy behind and go onto solid food (Hebrews 5:13-14). Just as natural children grow up and, hopefully, become friends of their parents, so we can become those Jesus refers to as his friends (John 15:15).

If we settle for a one-off experience then we will not grow into all that God has for us. His desire is that we are changed into the likeness of the perfect son, Jesus. This is part of our journey of walking with the Father.

Just as our journey into sonship is a progressive one, so too is our journey into freedom. When we become Christians we are set free from the eternal effects of sin and our future in Heaven is assured. But that does not mean that every area of our lives is suddenly set free. We still have to deal with our fallen nature and live in a fallen world. We are not suddenly given a ticket to a problem-free life. Unfortunately, things will still go wrong for us and for those we love.

In Romans 8 Paul tells us that the Spirit we have received is one of sonship which enables us to cry "Abba, Father" (Romans 8:15). By the work of the Holy Spirit we realise that we are neither slaves nor orphans but children of God. We have left our old life of slavery behind and have been brought into a freedom which comes from knowing that we are his sons and daughters. Not only are we children of God but we are also co-heirs with Jesus. Everything that belongs to Jesus now belongs to us! Paul certainly understood what Jesus was referring to in John 8.

There is a glory which will be revealed in us as we grow as sons and daughters - after all, we are being changed to be like Jesus. As the realisation of who we are grows within us so we grow into the "glorious freedom of the sons of God" (Romans 8:21). The ultimate expression of glory will be revealed in us once Jesus has come again, but we can start to experience this freedom **now**. The freedom which is on offer is a glorious one. It is not restricted to anything we can work up but it is the result of the Holy Spirit of sonship living within us.

In Romans 8:18-25 there is a sense of urgency. There is a groaning within us because we are desperately seeking and waiting for our adoption as sons. But Paul tells us that we have *already* received a spirit of sonship. In John 14, Jesus promises the Holy Spirit, who will live in us and take away our orphan heart. Paul is calling us away from a life of bondage and inviting us into a life of freedom, where we know that we are truly sons and daughters. This passage is making a prophetic declaration of the glory the Father sees in us and which he wants to be revealed through us, as we realise that we have received a spirit of sonship.

I have said that freedom is not a ticket to a problem-free life. It is, however, becoming free from sin, addiction and bondage. It is freedom from being dependent on the world's systems (be they financial, political or environmental). Our hearts can be free from the impact and destruction of the circumstances which may surround us.

As we grow as sons and daughters so the freedom we experience will also grow and become more evident in our lives. We weren't set free to remain captives. We were set free to experience real freedom, glorious freedom. As the sons of God are revealed there will be an impact on the world around us - on our families and on those with whom we work.

How then are the sons of God revealed?

I believe this 'revealing' happens as we are filled with his love and start to live as his children.

All those who receive Jesus have the right to become children of God (John 1:12) and are restored to sonship through Jesus' death and resurrection (Galatians 4:4-7). All Christians are sons or daughters of God but many still live as slaves or orphans. Somehow the truth has bypassed them. Jack Winter wrote: *"God did not love Jesus because he was perfect; he loved him because he was his son"*[3]. Of course, Jesus was perfect, but that was not the basis of the Father's love for him. It is the same for us. God does not love us because we are perfect, nor does he wait for us to become perfect; he loves us simply because we are his children.

As we receive a revelation of his love we will start to shine as the sons and daughters of God. Matthew 5:16 encourages us to let our light shine before men so that they may see our good deeds and give praise to our Father. This is not about other people seeing our polished performances but about the flow of his love through our lives which attracts others, not to us, but to our Father. As love flows through us, it will change us and flow from us to others. As we love others in the way we have been loved, the world will know that we are his disciples. We can only love others because he has first loved us! This is the hope for the world.

We are promised a *glorious* freedom. As with everything God offers, it is not a half measure. Our freedom will be attractive. Our freedom is meant to be un-bridled beauty.

This is our inheritance.

However, freedom is a choice. Whilst it is our birthright we can choose what we do with it. Adam and Eve lived in freedom before the Fall. As a result of the choice they made they lost their freedom. As we have seen, God never forces his will on us as that would not be true love, but manipulation or control. We too can live in freedom by choosing to lay aside the performance-oriented lifestyle we tend to pursue and instead become like Jesus. He knew he was loved and that the Father's favour was on him. His sole aim was to do his Father's will and he submitted joyfully. This was his life of freedom. It can be our choice too.

Christians talk a lot about the Kingdom of God or the Kingdom of Heaven. This was a major focus of Jesus' teaching and, it seems, something he was keen we should understand. I once heard it described as being like a bar of soap – when you think you've got hold of it, it just seems to slip away! However, I think it **is** something we can grasp. A king does not give his kingdom to slaves but to his heirs. He gives it to his sons and daughters. The Kingdom of God is a place where freedom reigns, as that is the nature of the Trinity. We will understand more of the Kingdom as we enter more fully into an intimate relationship with the Father as his sons and daughters. As we learn to live as the children of God we will understand more clearly what it means to be true citizens of that heavenly kingdom here on earth. When we start to leave our orphan ways behind and allow our lives to be filled with Father's love, we will leave a life of slavery and bondage and enter into the glorious freedom of the sons of God.

His Kingdom is our inheritance and it is a life of freedom!

We have glimpses of this throughout Scripture:

> "*He is wooing you from the jaws of distress to a spacious place free from restriction, to the comfort of your table laden with choice food.*" *(Job 36:16)*

> "*Even though I walk through the valley of the shadow of death, I will fear no evil, for you are with me, your rod and staff comfort me. You prepare a table before me in the presence of my enemies.*" *(Psalm 23:4-5)*

> "*One who breaks open the way will go up before them; they will break through the gate and go out. The king will pass through before them, the LORD at their head.*" *(Micah 2:13)*

God wants his children to break out and be free. He does not want us to live in a restricted place where we are unable to enjoy all that he has for us. He wants his glory to be revealed in us. He wants us to know that we are truly his sons and daughters. He wants us to glorify him through our lives. He wants us to separate ourselves from the world's orphan ways and leave them behind. The world is waiting for the sons of God to be revealed.

He offers us a life of freedom and it is ours to enjoy.

Notes:
1. *Homily in Orioles Park at Camden Yards - 8th October 1995, Pope John Paul II*
2. *Mike Tyson - Sports Illustrated March 1988*
3. *The Homecoming - page 188, Jack Winter*

Chapter 12

The Transforming Power of Love

"And so we know and rely on the love God has for us. God is love. Whoever lives in love lives in God, and God in him." (1 John 4:16 NIV)

Throughout this book I have tried to present the Father's love as simply as I can because I believe it is a simple thing.

As I have travelled in Africa and across Europe, I have met people with all sorts of backgrounds, upbringings and education. But what has struck me is that no one is prevented from coming to the Father. It is not dependent on education or where we fit into society. Whether we are poor or rich, whether we are highly educated or have only a simple understanding, we can all know that God is a Father to us. All it requires is a childlike understanding and simplicity of faith. I really believe that no one is barred from experiencing the Father's love and from knowing, in the depth of their heart, that they are his son or daughter.

I also know that there is no formula or switch we can flick to make us suddenly receive this extravagant love. Sometimes I wish there was!

I know people who have come almost instantly into a revelation and understanding of God's love but I also know some who have struggled for years to receive it. I know people who have tasted something, felt it was not for them at that time, and then, a few years later, have been bowled over by his love. I have, sadly, known people who reject the revelation of Father's love and carry on their Christian life seeking to be fruitful in their own strength.

I believe this revelation is for everyone. The fulness of God's goodness and love have not yet been revealed to the world. As we love one another as he has loved us, the world will start to see who he is. As we let him build the church, and take over our programmes and activities, the gates of Hell will not prevail against it. As we are revealed as the free sons of God, creation (including the people who are a part of it) will come into the same freedom. As we begin to enjoy the wide open pastures, people around us will be set free from their own captivity.

In learning to live in God's love we cannot rely on special occasions alone. Living in love is a lifestyle. As we live in love we allow its transforming power to change our hearts.

John encourages us to "live in love" (John 15:9), not to come in and go out as it suits us, but to dwell there permanently.

It is only as we live in love that we can come to know and rely on the love that God has for us (1 John 4:16). Those words "know" and "rely" are both experiential. These are not theoretical concepts but practical realities that affect us when we start to live in his love. "Knowing" means experiencing, touching, feeling or recognising. God's love is something we *know* because we have touched it and felt it. His love is something that affects every part of our lives. It is certainly not restricted to church activities for it is something which affects and changes our hearts. It is the day to day reality of his presence affecting everything we do. As we experience this love we can come to rely on it and know that it is steadfast and unshakeable.

Many of you will be familiar with the film "The Sound of Music" in which a young, attractive nun is sent to look after the children of a severe Navy captain. When Maria arrives in the house she is shocked to discover the harsh way in which this father treats his children. He uses a whistle when he wants them to come, issues orders and has them stand to attention. As the story unfolds we discover that the captain's wife has died and that he has closed his heart to love and feelings of any kind. Maria wins the hearts of the children and gradually starts to win the captain over as well. He changes from being a distant, harsh father to a gentle, loving one. He changes from being angry and intolerant to accepting his children with open arms. As Maria wins his heart he allows himself to be loved once again. This film is a wonderful story of the transforming power of love.

"The Sound of Music" shows us what the power of love can do. It illustrates what living in love means and how the Father's love can change us. As the captain received love he changed and he, too, became a lover. Just as Maria was persistent, so our Father is persistent in his pursuit of our hearts. As Maria brought life to a lifeless family, so the Father brings life to our lifeless hearts.

In the introduction I said that most of us know that God is a Father. I also pointed out that although many people know that I am a father, only my four children know it in a personal and experiential way. In this book I have sought to show that knowing God is a Father is not enough. What we need is a personal revelation of his extravagant love that changes our life from the inside out. In fact, a revelation of his love is not enough. What is really needed is an impartation of his love. As his very presence comes and fills us we will know that he really is loving us now! A revelation enables us to see something and it may change us for a while. An impartation involves a permanent change where God takes a part of himself, puts it in our hearts and we are changed forever. Going to a conference cannot be the beginning and end of this experience. It may be the start of a life-changing experience but we are called to live in love or, as another writer puts it, to make love our home.

What I have tried to show is that receiving the Father's love is not a one-off event. It is about living a life which is full of love. Of course we all leak, some faster than others, but we can keep coming back to be filled again with the extravagant and liberating love of the Father. Such a lifestyle is a progression where we change from one degree of glory to another. I encourage you never to tire of the process.

Just as Maria melted the Captain's heart so the Father wants to melt our hearts so they can be open to receive his love. His desire is that we know we are loved every moment of each day. We really can live loved! He wants us to know that his love is not dependent on our actions, abilities or performance. He loves us just because we are his sons or daughters. His love will change us. Over time it will transform our lives. It will work in our attitudes and in our actions. It will change our thoughts and motives. His love will change our relationships, our churches and, ultimately, I believe it will change our society.

The power of God's love will transform us and will keep on transforming us as long as we let it. God will never force himself into our lives. He waits till we open the door and let him in.

God wants us to know who he really is. For too long he has been misrepresented to the world and his true nature has not been made known. He does not want to stay shrouded in mystery and he certainly does not want to be known as distant or angry. He wants to reveal himself to us as he is.

God is a Father. He has always been a Father and he wants to be a Father to **YOU!**

Afterword

I am very grateful for two good friends, William Calvert and Mike Beaumont, who have been very thorough in their editing of this book and who have provided many helpful improvements to it. Thank you for taking the time and helping me on the journey. Thanks as well, to my friend Barry Adams for his encouragement to write the book and share the good news of Father's love.

Here are details of other resources you may want to look at as you live in the Father's love. Information about the week long schools run by Fatherheart Ministries can be found on the websites of *Fatherheart Ministries* or *Father's House Europe*.

A Father to YOU - www.afathertoyou.com
Audio and video teachings, teaching materials, inspirational videos and details of events in the UK.

The Father's Love Letter - www.fathersloveletter.com
An intimate message from God to you, in over 80 languages.

Fatherheart TV – www.fatherheart.tv
Inspirational videos and live webcasts to inspire and help you grow in the love of the Father.

Fatherheart Ministries – www.fatherheart.net
The ministry of James and Denise Jordan with
details of the International schools and other
events. Complete with online store with excellent
teaching resources.

Father's House Europe –
www.fathershouseeurope.com
Taking the revelation of the Father's love to
Europe. Also facilitating the European week long
schools – "Experiencing Father's Love". Online
store for teaching and other resources.